EVERYONE WILL
KNOW IT WAS GOD

SANA LATREASE

Everyone Will Know It Was God
Copyright © 2020 by Sana Latrease.

Published by :
Relentless Publishing House
www.relentlesspublishing.com

ISBN: 978-1-948829-71-7

10 9 8 7 6 5 4 3 2 1

TABLE OF CONTENTS

EVERYONE WILL
KNOW IT WAS GOD

Chapter One

E verybody get on the floor!" an officer yelled, after kicking down the door of my home in Bridgeport, Connecticut. My twin brother and I were around four years old when the police raided the crack house that we called home. We lived there with our mother and grandmother. I remember sitting there, aware. I wasn't scared or sad. I was simply aware. Aware of what had become normal for me. It wasn't the first time the crack house had been raided, and it certainly wouldn't be the last.

As they dragged away several people in handcuffs, I realized that my mother was one of them. Her eyes glazed over and blank, seemingly unaware that she was being arrested. My grandmother's arms wrapped tightly around my brother and me. Although she was high like my mother, she was alert enough to keep the police from taking us. The last officer sternly looked into my grandmother's vacant eyes. "Next time we'll be taking them with us," he declared, pointing to my brother and I. Just as fast as they invaded our "home", they were gone.

One would think that two four-year- old kids would have screamed and cried when the police dragged away our mother. However, we were numb to the trauma. Our mother had been in and out of prison multiple times. Our grandmother tried her best to fill in the gap when it was required, but she herself was battling an addiction also, and she was losing the battle.

There were days when we didn't eat. Days when the electricity was off, we lived in the dark for many days. Even though I was a little child, I had to learn to take care of us. There was a small grocery store across the street from the building we lived in on East Main Street. I remember the owner would allow me to sweep—I actually just dragged the broom across the floor— in exchange for peanut butter, jelly and bread. As much as I despise peanut butter and jelly now, I am thankful to that Puerto Rican man who recognized that we needed help and did what he could to lend a hand.

Unfortunately, the times we needed someone the most, no one was there. There were many men and women in and out of our home. My brother and I tried to stay out of the way, but we still fell prey to the strangers who moved around as if our home was their home. Many days, those men took advantage of me, stealing my innocence from me before I was aware of what it even was.

One day, late in the night, I heard a knock on the door. My grandmother opened it, and the police marched in like soldiers. One of them grabbed, me and the other scooped up my brother. I remember tears pouring from my eyes as I reached for my grandmother, begging her not to let them take us. My grandmother didn't react. She was still, staring into oblivion. High off a drug that meant more to her than the wellbeing of her only grandchildren. Police carried us out of the crack house and we went into the custody of the Department of Children and Families. Life as we knew it would never be the same.

The police dropped us off at Park City Hospital's emergency room where we remained for a few weeks, and then placed into the care of a foster family on the east end of Bridgeport. My little heart thumped rapidly in my chest as we pulled up to the house that would become our new home for the next few years. Walking up to the front door, my neck stretched back as I took in the massive house. My brother grabbed ahold of my hand and held it tightly. He looked at me, with his wild eyes filled with fear. In that moment, the protector innate in me, overpowered my fear. "Don't be scared. I'm going to take care of you, just like I always have," I promised him. Those words would end up sealing the nature of our relationship. My childlike mind transformed to that of an adult. My twin brother became my biggest responsibility. I vowed to take care of him and protect him from whatever harm life might bring.

Our social worker, Ms. Gay, walked us to the front door. When we reached the top step, the door flew open. Still holding hands, my brother and I scanned over the man and woman smiling down at us. The Morgans. They were the people who would introduce us to a new life.

The Morgans were a husband and wife that had recently started a church in the basement of their home. They had been foster parents for many years. They had also adopted quite a few children. The home was full of kids ranging from six-years-old to twenty-five-years-old. There was Melanie, Chris, Reva, Tiffany and now Sana and Javon.

Life with the Morgans was structured and strict. They were Christians so church was an important routine in the Morgan home. It was the Morgans who first introduced me to Christ and ministry. Each Sunday we would get ready for church and proceed to the basement for service. Although the service was held in their home, they had many members. Each of the Morgan children had a role to play in the church service, and Javon and I would be no different. My role was to be a junior usher and a choir member. We learned early on the importance of church and how to conduct ourselves while at church. Outside of church, Javon, Melanie and I were always together. Aside from karate class, we weren't part of any extracurricular activities. We created our own games to play around the house because the only room that had a TV was the Morgan's bedroom.

One day, Ms. Gay picked us up and took us to Storrs Correctional facility in Niantic, Connecticut to visit our birth mother. Although, I was comfortable and had adjusted well at the Morgan's home, I always hoped that my mother would get her life together and come back to get us. When we walked into the community room, it didn't feel like we were inside of a prison. Vibrant colors decorated the walls and lots of toys adorned the shelves. Many other children ran around joyfully, visiting their parents also. We dived into the fun, playing lots of games, getting our faces painted, doing arts and crafts, and taking smiley pictures with our moms. While eating lunch, we shared happy stories with our mom about our achievements in school. In the middle of chatting off our little faces, Ms. Gay walked over and hijacked our perfect day. "Alright, it's time to say goodbye," she told us. Caught up in the bliss of it all, we never stopped to consider that this time with our mother was temporary. A longing deep down in my stomach traveled up to my heart, crushing it until it shattered. Warm tears soaked my cheeks as I grabbed ahold of my mom, desperate for more time with her. My brother cried too. In fact, all the children began crying. The room erupted with screaming. Distraught moms frantically got in one last hug, wiping the tears from their babies eyes, clinging to the last bit of normalcy. Those car rides back home were the worst. No more excitement, no laughter just sniffles as we silently cried in the back seat. After a while, I started to dread those visits, knowing that they were only temporary and each visit would require me to leave a part of my heart in prison.

One Saturday, while playing a game of hide and seek with Javon and Melanie, the doorbell rang. Pausing my game, I went toward the door. "Who is it?" I asked. To my surprise, the voice on the other side of the door was my birth mother. I pulled open the door, ready to embrace her, but before I could get to her, my foster mother shut the door. "You can't be here. You need to leave, now," Mrs. Morgan told my birth mother from behind the closed door. I could hear my mother screaming on the other side. "I want my kids, give me back my babies." She must have screamed and cried, begged and pleaded, for what felt like hours while I begged to see my mother from the other side of the door. Eventually the banging and the screaming stopped, and my mother was gone. I often think of that day. As an adult, I realize that my mother may have been high during that time. There wasn't a drug strong enough that could stop her from locating and trying to get her babies back. The truth is that battle was one she was never meant to win. Not because she had been defeated by the enemy but simply because God needed me to win the war. A door is what separated the purpose of a mother and a child. As a mother succumbed to her purpose, a fire was being ignited on the inside of a daughter, and it all took place between a door. That would be the last time that I saw my birth mother as a child. Shortly thereafter, she relinquished her parental rights and I officially became a ward of the state.

As we continued life at the Morgan's home, there were many ups and downs, some of the other children may say more downs than ups, but everyone has their own experiences. Eventually, the Morgans outgrew the basement space in their home and acquired a church building not far from their home. They shared the space from time to time with another Pastor and First Lady who was also starting out in ministry.

One Sunday, I was sitting in church and happened to turn around. When I did, a bright light blinded me. The light was coming from two pews behind me. It turned out to be the sun coming from outside and shining on a little girl, but to my 7-year-old self, it felt like light radiating from an angel. I couldn't stop turning around in my seat to look into the face of this angel. Immediately after church, I went to speak to this angel. She was older than me by a year or two. I asked her name and she responded with, Sasha. I was in love. Something just drew me to her. I'd like to think it was the divine plan of God. Sasha was visiting the church with her siblings. I never knew why she came, but to this day, I believe God sent her just for me. For two weeks, I begged Mrs. Morgan for more time with Sasha. "Can we take her home? Please, can we take her home?" I pleaded. One Sunday we finally did, we took her home to live with us. Sasha's mother was going through a difficult

time and needed help with her children. Sasha was the oldest
and required less attention, so it made since for her to join our
large family. Sasha ended up playing a pivotal role in my life.
She spoiled me. She took me on her dates, she listened to me
speak my fears, she held me when I cried and calmed my very
soul. She literally protected me and became my rock.
Sasha was my angel.

Things began to get a little rocky in the Morgan home
not to long after that. Mr. and Mrs. Morgan began arguing
with each other often. Over time, the arguments became worse
and worse. One day, Mr. and Mrs. Morgan's voices boomed
throughout the house. They screamed at each other and called
each other names. Mr. Morgan ran for the door and Mrs.
Morgan was on his heels, taking the dispute outside. I watched
as Mr. Morgan tried to get into his car while arguing with his
wife. Mrs. Morgan peeled off her shoes and hauled them at
him. Eventually, Mr. Morgan got in his car and pulled off. We
never saw him again. We later found out that he had an affair
and Mrs. Morgan found out about the relationship. They
eventually divorced and that left Mrs. Morgan alone,
with health issues, still trying to care of her children and us.
During school vacations, she would have Javon and I go to
a babysitter's house during the day. The babysitter had two
teenage sons. I have tried for years to remember their names,
but have had no such luck. One of those brothers would molest
me every day we were there. I never told anyone because I

didn't want to be moved from the Morgan's home. Each day I would be dropped off knowing he would be molesting me under the cover while Javon and his brother were watching TV in the next room.

As Ms. Morgan's health began to decline, it was clear that she would not be able to keep my brother and me for much longer. Ms. Gay began to talk to us about a family that was interested in becoming our adoptive family. She wanted us to meet them and set up a date for us to visit. We visited the Mitchell family several times and I really liked them. I was beginning to feel that we would be okay if they adopted us.

That year, my life went through another shift. I went off to school with my siblings as I normally did. I waved goodbye to Sasha and then walked to Newfield elementary school. Around lunchtime, the school secretary called me down to the lunchroom. When I entered the lunchroom, I noticed that someone had decorated for a party. Bright colored balloons graced the room and gifts were on the table. I started wondering why they had called me to the lunchroom. My 8th birthday wasn't for another few months, so surely this was not my birthday. I looked around the room perplexed until my social worker, Ms. Gay, walked into the room. "Surprise!" she sang out. "This is your going away adoption party."
"Huh? Adoption party?" I asked, still greatly confused. "Yes," she stated. Today you're going to live with your new family, the Mayfield's.

I never got to go back to the Morgan's home. I never said a final goodbye to Sasha. I never said goodbye to the Morgan kids. They placed me in the car where all of my clothes were already packed and, in the trunk, and away we went. Next stop, New Britain, CT.

REFLECTIONS:
God Doesn't Disqualify

Many of us can relate to experiencing a traumatic childhood. For me, my mother's drug addiction set in motion a cascade of challenges—separation from my family of origin, living in multiple homes, exposure to sexual predators, and many other challenges that I will share in the pages to follow. In general, our childhoods are a catalyst to who we become as adults. For me that was certainly the case. I plan to share my life story with you from childhood to adulthood. A story that—in theory—should have broken me. I don't want you to feel bad for me while reading my story. What I want you to do is pay attention to God's hand and how He works strategically. Pay attention to how He orchestrated great things for me while I was in the midst of uncomfortable hurt. Though many things happened to me and around me, it didn't disqualify me from God's love or His purpose for my life. I want you to know that no matter what happened in your life. You are loved by God. Your life has purpose. Your life is a journey that is ultimately about believing in God and believing that He created you because your existence is necessary in this world.

God's purpose for your life doesn't change because bad things happen to you.

Chapter Two

New Britain, Connecticut would be the next place that I called home. William and Alberta Mayfield would become my new parents. The Mayfield's already had a son together, and Mr. Mayfield had four children from previous relationships. They were interested in having another daughter and felt that adoption would be the best route. Mr. Mayfield had been adopted so the choice to adopt was close to his heart. While searching through the adoption books, they came across the profile of my brother and I. They seemed to have fallen in love with my infectious smile and my bright personality radiating from the page. At least, that's the joke I like to tell. A more accurate version of the story would likely include divine intervention. Our story immediately touched their heart, and although they were only looking to adopt one child, they adopted both of us. When our birth mother gave up her rights, she made a request for my twin brother and I not to be split up, and they obliged.

Our home on Judd Ave was a modest three-bedroom apartment, but it was an exciting new beginning for us. That

modest home was where many of my memorable childhood
firsts would occur. For the first time ever, I got to have my own
room. The boys shared a room together, while I got to spread
out in my very own space. My room was every
little girl's dream. It was full of interesting books to delight my
imagination. The cabbage patch dolls and Barbies kept my
seven-year-old self busy being mother as I filled their bellies
with nonexistent food and tucked them close to me at night.
For the first time, I felt like a precious little girl. I felt as if
someone cared enough for me to give me a place to dream, a
place where I could sleep peacefully and protected. That room
was my heaven, my place of solitude.

While inside of my room was my place to dream freely,
outside of my room our strict foster parents ran a very
structured home. We went to school. Came straight home to
have a snack and do homework. Then we would have dinner,
followed by taking out our clothes for the next day. We'd have
to get a shower, and then spend an hour together watching
family television programming. We would end our day with
prayers and then bedtime. We would wake up the next day and
do it all over again. During the weekend, we did chores on
Saturday mornings and ran errands or we would do a family
activity. On Sundays, we went to church ALL day. Church and
God was very important in the Mayfield home, which wasn't
anormal to me because it was the same in the Morgan home as
well. We attended prayer service, bible study and choir

practice during the week, every week. On most Saturdays, the boys would spend the day at the Boys Club, which is now known as the Boys & Girls Club. My foster mom and I would spend the day doing girl things like, going to the hair salon, and shopping. On those days I kept quiet and to myself, refusing to allow myself to smile and enjoy quality time with my foster mom. As I look back, I really wish I would have valued that time with her. Spending girl time with me was her way of trying to establish a bond. Even though I enjoyed going shopping and getting my hair done, there was a part of me that felt like if I enjoyed those moments too much, I was being disloyal to my birth mom. You see, my birth mom was the one I dreamed about having an unbreakable bond with. I wished that she was the one who wanted to treat me to a day of shopping and laughs, and my heart wouldn't allow me to replace her. I was scared that having too much fun with my foster mother would cause me to forget my birth mom. My heart still hoped that she would get her life together and come back and get us. I prayed for the stability and normalcy that I felt in the Mayfield home—the three-bedroom home, my own room, the family time—but I wanted it with our birth mother instead. I soon realized that the hopes and prayers were empty. Those hopes would never be reality. Our birth mother had signed over her rights. We were officially wards of the State of Connecticut. That meant that there was no way we were going back to live with her.

Another first I experienced while living with
the Mayfield's was that I was able to meet my very first friends,
one of which became my best friend. I shared thing with them
that I never shared with anyone else. They knew my fears; the
things that kept me up at night. They knew about my dreams
of living with my birth mother again. They got to see how silly I
could be when I freed all my inhibitions. Those girls were
literally my walking diaries. Whenever I had a little bit of
freedom, I wanted to spend every drop of that time with my
besties.

In October of 1990, I had the biggest first of my life. It was
my first birthday party, and I was turning 8 years old. I was
over the moon with excitement. The theme of the party was
Barbies and Ninja Turtles. My brother and I each had our own
cake and all of our new friends were there to celebrate us. They
belted out the birthday song while my brother and I smiled
from ear to ear. Candles lit up our little faces as we anticipated
blowing them out after making a wish. That day seemed like
there was nothing more in the world to wish for. We had our
friends to play games with. When we finished the games, we
danced to music, waving our hands in the air and throwing our
bodies around in silly childlike fashion. We laughed and smiled
more than we ever had. As an adult, I still look back on that day
and remember it as one of the best days of my life. People fail
to realize that things that most people take for granted like
birthdays are cherished to foster kids. They are moved around

so often that they don't get the opportunity to have celebrations or be celebrated through birthday parties. My first birthday party is a memory that I will never forget. To this very day, I always make sure that I give my kids a big birthday party every year. Not because they're spoiled children, but simply because I desire to give to them what my foster parents gave to me at my first and to this day, only, birthday party— laughter and memories that will last a lifetime.

My life truly began to change during the first year with my new foster family. The Mayfield's introduced me to many new experiences, but my heart was still with the Morgan's. I missed them every day, especially Sasha. She and I would write letters back and forth for a while when I first left, and sometimes she would call and check in on me. Eventually, as I settled into life with my new family and communication with Sasha ceased. Bridgeport seemed so far away from where I was currently living. The effects of being taken from my birth family, and then placed with a second family, and then replaced with a third family hit me like a ton of bricks. I started doing things just for attention. One day, crept into my foster parents' room and went through her stuff. I discovered my foster mom's little bottles of perfume and I stole them. I gave them away at summer camp for no good reason. I found myself having horrible mood swings. One moment I would be happy and full of life and then the next minute I would be angry and not want to be bothered with anyone. Altercations between my foster mom and I began to occur because I just didn't know how to channel my feelings. She seemed like the most appropriate person to take out my anger on. I would scream at her, saying the most horrible things. Somedays when I was feeling completely out of control, I would go as far as literally fighting her. I couldn't comprehend what was triggering me to make me do those things. However, I could feel the hollowness inside of me. It was a feeling so excruciating that it was impossible to ignore. My pain couldn't be put into words. It was like my young mind knew that I had been displaced in the world, but no one could find me to place me back where I belonged. I couldn't figure out why my birth mother didn't love me enough to care for me and nurture like a mother is supposed to. The truth is, I would search most of my life for that type of nurturing, but no woman would ever be able to fulfill it.

There was so much that I wanted to say about how I was feeling, but I didn't have an outlet. Therefore, I processed everything in my head. I would just shut down. When I tried to sleep, I would have nightmares. Meanwhile, my brother was struggling in his own ways. He would wet the bed or hide his food in plastic bags around the house. He had developed a bad stutter and was struggling in school. He would sit at the table for hours trying to finish his homework each night while I breezed through mine. Seeing him like that affected me even more, especially since I promised to take good care of him. Even though we were the same age, I tried to fill the motherly void for him. Mrs. Mayfield would have to constantly remind me that I was not his mother. She was now, and I needed to allow her to parent him. It was one of the hardest things to do as I had been assuming the role of his mother for years. I was the one constant person that he could depend on, and I took my role very serious. This caused a bit of conflict between me and my new foster mother and in my opinion set the foundation for what would become an awkward relationship in the future.

A little over a year after experiencing my first birthday party, I experienced another unforgettable day. It was a day that many foster kids dream of—adoption day. On December 3, 1991, we arrived at the Berlin Probate District Court in New Britain, Connecticut on a beautiful day. The day wasn't beautiful because of the weather. The sun wasn't shining, but to me it was the brightest day of my life because it was the day that I would officially have a forever family. It was actually freezing that day. The temperature was around forty-seven degrees and it was cloudy, but there was so much love and warmth in the judge's chambers of the courthouse. Even though I had been experiencing a rollercoaster of feelings, that day I was so excited to officially become a part of a family. As we sat before the judge in his chambers, he began to ask us about our life with the Mayfield's.

"Are you sure you want the Mayfield's to adopt you?" the judge asked in a kind yet serious tone.

I remember looking up at the ceiling as I pondered his question. The realization of what was about to happen began to sink in. If I said yes, that meant officially letting go of my birth mother. If I said no, I would continue to be displaced, without a family to call my own. A huge part of me wanted to run out of there and continue waiting for my birth mom to come get me. Subconsciously, I knew that wasn't going to happen.

"Yes," I finally responded in a small voice, deciding to accept my life with the Mayfield's because honestly, it was a good life. I just couldn't deny or shake the longing I felt for the woman who gave birth to my brother and I.

"Would you like to change your name?" he fired another question at me.

I needed no time at all to think about the answer to that question. "Yes," I replied quickly, sure of myself.

I certainly wanted to change my name. My birth name was so long! Sana Amenta Doris Choice had to go! Because I wasn't expecting to have the opportunity to change my name, I didn't have a new name picked out. I knew I didn't want to change my first name because everyone knew me by Sana. I couldn't image being called anything else as a first name, but my middle and last name could definitely be changed. My older cousin, Delita began to throw out different possible names. I didn't like any of them. "How about Sana Latrease?" Delita suggested and it was like a beautiful melody to my ears. I fell in love with that name. Latrease, it fit me. Sana Latrease Mayfield was officially born.

REFLECTION:

The Rebirthing Season/ Starting Anew

God takes each and every one of us through a process of rebirth at some point in our lives. This process is never pretty. It's almost always painful to the point the point of no return, because that's the goal—to never return. Suffering can become a crutch, and although we know we're merely surviving instead of thriving, we cling on to the suffering because at least it's familiar. As a kid, I didn't understand that I was barely surviving when I was with my birth mom. God had to pluck me out of that situation because it would have killed me. And even though I was safe, well fed, and thriving at the Mayfield's, I craved the familiar, which was death instead of life. God needed me to discover life anew in Him. That process would become a long and agonizing undertaking, but He had to start somewhere. My rebirthing season was upon me. It was the beginning of me unlearning who I had been in order for me to learn what God had designed for my life. If you in a season where you feel pain to the point of no return, consider that perhaps God plan isn't for you to return. Maybe God needs you to unlearn who you have been so that He can birth something new in you.

Chapter
Three

In the summer of 1994, our family moved from New Britain, Connecticut to Middletown, Connecticut. My parents purchased their first home and we were so excited to move in. The house was beautiful. My favorite part was the front door which was painted red. Our house was the only house in the neighborhood with a red door, which made our home stand out and feel special. My parents furnished the entire house with new furniture. I moved into a new room. It was even more fabulous than the one I fell in love with previously. It was located across the hall from my parent's room, which meant that although I had my own room, my parents were literally a few feet away and that brought me comfort.

I was eleven years old and headed into the sixth grade at a new school. My eyes shifted nervously as I looked at the hundreds of unfamiliar faces. It was my first day at the new school in a new town. I crossed my arms over my chest, insecure about the womanly assets I had developed at the tender age of twelve and dragged my feet into the building. As I stepped into the building, butterflies fluttered in my stomach. With the flutters wreaking havoc inside me, I desperately glanced around for a friendly face. Many of the kids seemed to know each other from previous years, while I stood searching for a kindhearted soul to befriend. Two girls smiled at me. Their names are Takesha and Cozette. We instantly became friends, and then upgraded to best friends shortly after. Our personalities meshed well together and those two girls are still my two best friends over twenty years later. With Kesha and Cozy, I was finally able to be myself. I didn't have to pretend. I could just be Sana and they loved me for who I truly was.

I excelled in school. My grades were one area that I always handled effortlessly. My parents never had to worry about my homework or my behavior in school. I tried my hardest to behave at home as well. I kept up on my chores religiously and I tried to keep my mouth under control because I didn't want my adoptive parents to send me to another home. The fear of moving yet again, having to restructure my life, and having to adjust to a new family was real. Stability wasn't normal for me even though I craved it. Therefore, I did my best to keep it together externally, but inside, I was losing my mind. My heart ached tremendously from the void of my birth family. I just didn't fit in with my adoptive family and I found myself daydreaming about fitting in perfectly with birth family, like a missing piece to a puzzle. Sitting in my room, I often thought about where they were or what they were doing. On holidays, I would imagine a large group of beautiful black people gathered around a long table, laughing loudly and lovingly as they ate a good meal. I could see them in my head making memories as a lovingly family, but I wasn't there. I was in my room, sad and alone. As bad as I wanted to share my feelings with my adopted parents or family, I never wanted to feel ungrateful, or disloyal. However, the truth was, no matter how good they were to me, they could never fulfill my longing for looking into the face of people who shared my features, who had the same mannerisms, and who's bodies held the same blood.

One day my mom called my brother and I into her room. As we entered her room, we could sense the seriousness in her composed body language. "I need to talk to you guys about something important," she said, directing us to sit on the edge of her bed.

We sat down and intensively listened as she spoke. "Aunt E called me from prison," she began. "She told me that there is a woman in there with her who keeps talking about her set of twins that had been removed from her custody"

My heart started pounding in my chest as I began to piece together the story in my head. Hanging on the edge of her bed, anticipating hearing more.

"The daughters name was Sana," she looked at me pointedly. "I'm certain that she's your birth mother," she finally revealed, telling me exactly what I wanted to hear. "She is very sick."

My birth mother had been diagnosed with Aids and was dying. A few weeks later, we found ourselves headed to York Correctional Facility to see our birth mom for the first time since we were 6 years old.

When pulled up to the prison, memories began to flood my mind from years before. I could feel a sense of familiarity. I remembered the earlier years when we visited our mom along with many other foster children coming to visit their moms. I could picture the vibrant colors, the games, and the face painting in the community room. This time was quite different though. They didn't usher us into a colorful room. They searched us thoroughly as we went through several barriers of security. Nothing about the experience was vibrant or fun, in fact, the walls were grey and dull. The lights were dim, and there was a plexie glass separating us. As I anxiously awaited my mother's arrival, I had so many questions that I wanted to ask. I was extremely excited but tried to hide my excitement as best I could so that my adopted mother wouldn't feel bad. However, I was bouncing inside as I looked through the glass that separated us, waiting for her to appear. Those short minutes felt like years as I waited, and then she finally rounded the corner. My wide eyes soaked her in as she walked forward in her prison issued uniform. She was stunning, despite her condition and the uniform. Her short stature perfectly complimented her shapely attributes, and her face was striking. If I could have, I would have jumped through that glass and embraced her. She sat down and I examined every inch of her face, unable to remove my eyes from her. As I looked her over, I realized that her face looked almost identical to mine. I looked more like my mother than I did my twin brother. As she began to speak, she wanted to know everything about us. She had a ton of questions and I had a ton of answers. I couldn't even think of any of the questions I had mentally prepared to ask her. All of those days I obsessed over being able to have time with her, she was in front of me but my brain was too amped up to process it. I was just excited to see her face and hear her voice. An hour later, our visiting time had come to an end. We held on to those last seconds, utilizing every moment until they disconnected the intercom. We said our goodbyes, promising to write each other and stay in contact. The moment my mother got up off her stool and started walking away, my tears stared flowing. I wouldn't turn my head until I could no longer see her anymore. As we drove back home those feelings of abandonment reared its ugly face. It was a feeling that I had grown to get accustomed to and I didn't like it.

My mother and I wrote letters back and forth for the next few months. She became my new personal diary. I shared everything that I was going through in my letters. I told her about my first crush, my grades, arguments with my parents, activities at school—everything. I couldn't wait to get home from school and check the mailbox. From those letters my mother did the only parenting she could. She gave me advice, scolded me when I wasn't doing my best at school, and always told me how proud of me she was. Those next few months went by quickly and before I knew it, my mother was released from prison.

After my mother was released, my adopted mother and my birth mother came to an agreement, deciding that it would be okay for her to come and pick my brother and I up every other weekend. Each week, I would make sure that my homework was done, my chores were completed, and I kept my attitude to myself. I didn't want anything to hinder me from being able to go with my mother for the weekend. When Friday came, I anxiously anticipated her car pulling in front of our home. When she arrived, I darted out of the door and into her car. I couldn't get out the house fast enough. As we got in the car, my mother introduced us to a friend of hers. His name was Lambert. He was very quiet, but very affectionate toward my mother. I could see how much he loved her just by the way he looked at her. As we drove into Bridgeport, I peered out of the backseat window, taking in the huge city that I was born in. The place where I took my first breath. My eyes danced over the bright lights and the sky-scraping buildings. With wind blowing through my hair, I hung out of the window listing to the city's hustle and bustle— the honking vehicles and the conversations at the corner stores. I was in love. I felt like I finally fit in. It was hard to wrap my brain around the fact that I was finally going home after all the tears, tantrums, and trials. After dreaming about this moment for so many years, it was finally happening. We arrived at the house where our mother was staying and introduced to her friends Debbie and Allen who we were to call Aunt Debbie and Uncle Allen. I never found out how my mother knew them; we were just told that they were family. As we got settled in the house and waited for Lambert to bring us dinner, I noticed several medicine bottles of all sizes on my mom's dresser. My mom caught me eyeing the pill bottles curiously and began to explain that she had to take those various pills due to her Aids. She literally took pills every day, multiple times a day. It was in that moment that I realized the life my mother had lived. It wasn't a good life by any means. I couldn't begin to imagine what circumstances in her life led her to her current situation. During our weekend visits, we had the opportunity to meet other members of our birth family, which I absolutely loved getting to meet family and spend time with them. We met many of our cousins, out maternal grandfather, and many of their close friends. One weekend, our mother took us to one of her friend's house. She said that she had to run an errand and that she would be right back. We sat on the couch in her friend's living room, looking around as the place was foreign to us. At first, we waited with patience, however, the more hours that passed by, the more our anxiety grew. After several hours, our mother still had not returned. My brother and I decided to leave. We walked out of the house and wandered around in the unfamiliar city until we found a pay phone on the corner. We called our adoptive mom and our maternal grandfather. Our grandfather picked us up and took us home. That was the last time we seen or heard from our mother alive.

REFLECTIONS:
Coincidence or God-incidence.

As I said previously, I do not want you to feel bad for me when I'm telling you about how I cried alone in my room, longing deeply for my birth mother, so much so that my heart physically hurt. I simply want you to recognize the hand of God and how He works strategically. I want you to pay attention to how he orchestrated great things for me when I couldn't fathom that anyone loved me, let alone my Heavenly Father.

Let's go back to how my adopted aunt just "happened" to be in jail with my birth mother. My aunt and my birth mother were from two different cities. They had never crossed paths with each other before meeting in prison. Add in my birth mother confiding in my aunt about how she missed her twins that she lost to the foster system many years prior. My birth mother didn't know that the woman she was confiding in knew exactly where her children were and could put her in direct contact with them. There is no way that anyone could justify that as a coincidence. In fact, there are no coincidences in God's kingdom, only perfectly orchestrated blueprints to get you exactly where God needs you to be. Have enough faith to trust that God is working in your life, even if you can't see it right now.

*There are no coincidences in
God's kingdom.*

Chapter Four

After I had gotten a taste of the town where I was born and where my birth family lived, I couldn't get it out of my system. I had grown into a teenager and started wanting more freedom. I had never felt freer than when I was in Bridgeport. In my freshman year of high school, I began working a babysitting job in a neighborhood close to my house. While there, I would use their phone and telephone book to find the numbers of my birth family listed in the white pages. After a few weeks, I was able to get in touch with my grandfather again. I told him how much I missed him and how suffocated I felt in my current home and city. We began making plans for him to come pick me up a few weeks after I finished, my freshman year, which would be the beginning of my summer vacation. The plans were set, but I never cleared my plans with my adoptive parents. As freshman year slowly came to an end, I began packing my clothes in trash bags, ready for my summer of freedom. When the date that my grandfather and I discussed finally arrived, I crept stealthily to backyard and hid my packed bags. I did my chores, got myself dressed, and before I knew it, I heard the doorbell ringing throughout the house. Knowing that it was my grandfather, I began making my way toward the door. My mom made her way toward the door also. When she pulled opened the door, she found my grandfather and birth aunt standing on the other side. She looked at them with a perplexed expression, quite surprised to see them at her home. My aunt began to explain that they were there to pick me up for the summer because I had called them. My mother was growing more and more upset by the minute, but she held it inside. "Once you leave, you better not ever think you're coming back," my mother said with calm resolve. I began putting my garbage bagged clothes into my grandfather's car. I said bye to my mother, and we left. Just like that, I had essentially ended a relationship with the woman and family who had chosen me out of a book of children to be their very own. I left alone. Without the one person who came into this world with me, my twin brother.

When we arrived in Bridgeport, my grandfather and aunt decided that my Aunt Lisa had the best accommodations for me. She had a house on the north end, which had room for me to stay. A few different people lived with my aunt at the time. She had two young daughters, another niece, Ronisha, and her mother all lived with my Aunt Lisa. Ronisha was a few years older than me, and I fell in love with her essence and the way she lived her life. She was a hairdresser who was highly gifted. She was driven, determined, and had a plan for her life. She had the coolest group of friends. Ronisha would let me hang with her and her friends whenever I wanted. When I wasn't hanging with Ronisha, I spent my time at my Aunt SG's house on the west side of Bridgeport. SG had six kids—four boys and two girls. I was close in age with her daughters, Shana and Yvonne, and we hit it off immediately. SG looked a lot like my birth mother, which meant I looked a lot like her. Most people thought I was also her daughter. There were many kids who were my age on Lenox Ave, the street SG and her family lived on. Naturally, I gravitated toward being around the kids my age, so I found myself staying with SG most days. We would have a ball. People watching from the front porch, making jokes, laughing, tons of walks to the corner store or Chinese restaurant, attending house parties and staying up all night. I have a ton of memories from that summer on Lenox Ave. Since I was a new face, I received lots of attention from some of the older guys. I was mature both physically and mentally for my age so most of them thought I was older than I actually was at the age of 15. One day my cousin informed me that one of her boyfriend's friends was interested in me. His name was Rashid. Rashid was very quiet, always well dressed, and driving a different car. He never hung around when he came by. If he came for a particular reason, he would handle his business and then leave, which meant he was only around for a few minutes. I had saw him come by the house only a few times. He said hi to me, but that was it. He never started a conversation with me or gave me any indication that he was interested in me. Therefore, I was surprised to hear that he noticed me at all. One evening, after a house party, Yvonne and I were walking home when a car crept up alongside of us. The driver rolled down their window, and it was Rashid. "Do y'all need a ride home?" he asked us.

"Yea," Yvonne and I gladly accepted the ride.

"You can sit in the front seat," he offered, looking directly at me. I hopped up front and we were on our way back to Lenox Ave. Rashid was completely silent the whole way there. The music was on, but if it hadn't been, you could have heard a pin drop. When we pulled up to the house, there was a crowd of people that had gathered to watch a fight that started at the house party. Yvonne got out of the car and walked toward the house, as I opened my door, Rashid stopped me. "You want to chill with me for a little while?" he asked shyly.

His question caught me off guard so it took me a minute to process my thoughts and come up with an answer. "Sure, I'll chill," I answered with a shrug of the shoulders. I closed my door and slid low in my seat because I didn't want anyone to see me leave with him. We rode around for a little while in awkward silence until we eventually pulled up to a house. I assumed it must have been his home since he had a key and let himself in. I followed him to a bedroom where he proceeded to turn on the TV. Finally, he began talking more. He asked me a few questions about myself. I answered the question and in turn asked him a few questions about himself. He gave me short responses and one-word answers. Before I knew it, we were kissing. I remember seeing the black and white static coming from the TV screen because the movie he turned on had ended. That night, I lost my virginity to Rashid. After we were done, I sat up, put on my clothes in a hurry and ran out the door. I kept running until I arrived back on Lenox Ave. I finally stopped running when I was safely sitting in the back stairwell of the house. That is when the sobbing started. I was scared because my mind wasn't mature enough to comprehend what had just happened. I knew that I felt disgusting, exposed, and hallow inside. Sex was not what I imagined. It wasn't romantic, it wasn't beautiful, in fact, it hurt. After that night, I refused to speak to Rashid. He would come by the house and I would hide. If I ran into him while I was out, I would act as if I didn't see him. I wasn't mad at him. I was just embarrassed. Eventually, he stopped trying to speak to me and we just moved on as if nothing ever happened. In hindsight, I believe that was the moment when I knew sex would become something that I honestly could do without. That moment shaped my view on sex and unearthed memories from year's prior—memories that I had buried deep down. The memories of being molested and engaging in an act that wasn't pleasing to me came flooding back, pulling me underwater and stealing my youthful spirit.

When the summer ended, my adopted mom had begun calling my grandfather questioning what day he was bringing me home since school would be starting soon. I honestly never had any intentions of going back. My plan was to stay and enroll into a school in Bridgeport and start a new life. Unfortunately, my grandfather thought it would be better if I went back home for school and came back on the weekends. I think he realized that I was beginning to spiral out of control, and he wanted better for me. Two weeks before school started, I headed back home to Middletown, back to a life that I knew I would never fit into again.

As I entered my parents' house after ten weeks of vacation, I felt like a different person. I had grown and had experiences of my own that summer. The old Sana who stayed in the house following a strict regimen had been replaced by Sana who stayed up all night and attended house parties. To be frank, I dreaded going back to my old life. However, I did look forward to seeing my brothers. I missed them. I brought all my stuff into the house and looked around for my twin. "Where's Javon?" I asked when I didn't see him with the rest of the family.

"He's gone," one of my family members, answered.

"Gone where?" I questioned, growing annoyed by the evasive answer.

"He's in prison," someone finally told me. Apparently, he had been there for a few weeks. My heart felt like it had dropped out of my chest and splattered on the floor. Everyone else seemed completely nonchalant about it. I sat there for a second and let it sink in. My twin brother, born two minutes after me, the one who I had taken on the responsibility to protect since we were removed from our birth mother's custody was gone. I felt like I had failed him. I had left him there alone, and now he was gone.

The next few weeks went by quickly and it was time for me to go back to school. I was entering my sophomore year of high school. During school, I was able to escape and keep myself sane. On the surface, my friends saw me smiling the smile that shrunk my eyes and showed all fifty-three of my pearly white teeth. My teachers saw me putting in the work to keep up my good grades. On the way home from school, I would happily sing along with the latest R&B hits that came on my CD player while on the back of the bus, but when I got home, my smile faded. I felt trapped and alone. I cannot reiterate enough that my parents were good people. I just didn't feel like I was a part of the family. They were super strict, and I felt like I didn't have room to be me. Not to mention, I was angry that they had allowed the police to come and take my brother and put him in jail. Because of this, I just didn't want to be bothered. I became disrespectful. I would say things like, "You're not my real mother anyways." I even went as far as physically fighting my mother on multiple occasions. My anger was always directed at my mother. It wasn't until I became much older that I realized why I directed my anger at her. She was trying to assume a role, but my heart didn't have any room for her. The only room in my heart at that age was for my family of origin as I struggled to find my footing in life. I knew that I couldn't stay in that house much longer. I was miserable, and I wanted to go back to the one place that I felt free, with the people that I felt my freest with, in Bridgeport with my birth family.

REFLECTIONS:
You Have Choices

It was my choice to leave my home in Middletown and run the streets of Bridgeport. The night I laid down on that bed and painfully lost my virginity, it was a choice that I had made. No, I didn't anticipate how empty and devalued it would make me feel, but because I made the choice, I suffered the consequences.

We all have choices to make in our lives. We get to choose if we're going to allow life's difficulties and disappointments to define who we ultimately become. When I decided to go along with Rashid, I was letting life's disappointments define me. I never felt love from my mother, so the attention from a boy gave me hope that I was loveable. Somewhere deep down inside my mind, I had already decided that I wasn't worthy of love or a relationship. The biggest piece of wisdom that I can impart from that night and pass on is never make a choice based on your current circumstance. Always look to your future with an expectation of greater. You have the choice to accept life as it is or choose to change it. You won't always be able to control difficult circumstances, but you can always control how you react to those circumstances. You have power over your actions, beliefs, and choices.

Never make a decision based on your current situation.

Chapter
Five

With everything that I was dealing with at home and within myself, school became my safe haven. It was the one place where I could forget my troubles and focus on what made me happy, kept me feeling upbeat, and what kept me smiling. I submerged myself into anything that was positive at school, creating good bonds with my friends and taking advantage of the opportunities the school offered. My Technical Highschool had added Culinary Arts as an elective that year so that was the trade that I chose to focus on. Cooking was one of the things that made me happy, so I dived in.

That year, I befriended a freshman guy who was almost a male version of myself. His name was Anthony. Anthony and I clicked immediately, bonding over being church kids with strict parents. Anthony was always outgoing and kind of a flirt in school. The upper classmen thought he was just a cute, annoying, freshman kid, and no one really took his flirting serious. One day while waiting for the school busses at dismissal there was a loud commotion. Anthony and I were talking and laughing like normal when a boy named Jason interrupted us. Jason was a young man who was also in my sophomore class. He approached Anthony, towering over him with a scowl on his face. "You better stay out of Tasha's face," Jason threatened in a booming voice.

Anthony was a fun-loving kid, not a fighter so he immediately began to draw back. "I don't know what you're talking about," Anthony assured him, the fear apparent in his tone.

However, Jason was relentless. He kept questioning Anthony about Tasha. Anthony told Jason repeatedly that he didn't do anything. Before we could do anything, Jason punched Anthony and didn't stop punching him until Anthony fell to the ground. The punching turned into violent kicking, repeatedly. Anthony tried his hardest to fight back, but he didn't stand a chance. Jason was at least twice his size in weight and height. I frantically searched the crowd, screaming for help until my throat was raw. I was looking for someone— anyone—to help stop the violent fight happening before our eyes, it dawned on me that in the sea of a couple of hundred kids, not one person was willing to stop the fight. I began pushing Jason away from Anthony, begging him through my sobs to stop. Anthony was barely moving, covered in dirt, and his own blood. By the time the staff arrived, Anthony was almost unconscious. Anthony was so hurt that he had to be taken to the hospital in an ambulance. The school called the police, and they called me to the principal's office as a witness. I had me write a statement. As I sat in the office, waiting for my mother to pick me up, since I had missed the bus, I remember thinking to myself that this is entirely too much. This young man had almost lost his life and no one—not one person—came to his rescue. It made me sick to my stomach. It became a life altering moment for me. My heart had been touched and it was alive. A heavy sense came over me, letting me know that there was more to my life. I wanted to be someone who helped others, not the person standing around watching. Unfortunately, that person was still in development. God had a long way for me to go before I was able to get off my rollercoaster of emotions to focus on anyone other than myself.

A few weeks after that incident occurred, I contacted my grandfather and asked him to come back and get me. I was ready to officially move to Bridgeport. This time I let my parents know that I was leaving. My mother in a very calm tone, "If you don't want to be here, then go," she said, resolved. That is exactly what I did. I moved in with my aunt and began living what would be my new life. It was definitely completely different from what I was used to. I didn't have to go to school. No one badgered me about doing chores. I didn't have to ask anyone for permission to do anything. I was living my best life at the age of 16. At least I was naïve enough to think that I was living my best life.

My older cousin ended up getting pregnant with her first child not to long after moving in with my aunt. Since she hadn't finished high school, she decided to go to Job Corps and try to get her GED before the baby arrived. Since I hadn't finished school yet either, and she didn't want to go alone, I decided to go with her. I convinced my aunt's boyfriend to pretend that he was my father so he could sign me out of my old high school and get a copy of my transcripts. He was able to get the transcripts, enabling my aunt to sign me into Grafton Job Corps, located in North Grafton, Massachusetts.

As soon as I entered Job Corps, it was very easy for me to pass the educational requirements. I passed my GED within the first week of being there. Once I had my GED, they enrolled me in their culinary program. The culinary program was very disorganized, making it difficult for me to maintain focus. I found myself board and searching for other things that would keep my attention. I began befriending the plethora of people who attended Job Corps from the surrounding cities and states—Rhode Island, Massachusetts, New York, New Jersey, and several others. This was finally my opportunity to be myself, as I so badly wanted to be without any parental or familial pressure or support. I instantly went into survival mode, creating my own family whom I can depend on for support. The people that I met became my extended brothers, sisters, and mentors who felt like parents. Then I met Jeffrey. Jeffrey was my own personal DMX—rough around the edges, a hustler, but so incredibly wise. Jeffrey easily won my heart. He was the first person that I felt genuinely saw me from the inside out. He understood my hurt and encouraged me to be resilient. He saw beyond my face and body, appreciating my heart and loving my soul. Although, we never entered a sexual relationship, we connected deeply on a mental level. Jefferey was the one who taught me how important it was to love, honor, and respect a man that EARNED it. He taught me about pride, fear, the streets and most of all, he taught me about ME, Sana. Jeffery helped me see the power that I had within myself. He ending up leaving Job Corps, and taking a piece of my heart with him. However, I would take with me the seeds of wisdom he planted within me for years to come.

After Jeffrey left, I had a hard time continuing with Job Corps. My heart just wasn't in it anymore. I would cry all day and stay in my dorm waiting for a call from him. My girls did their best trying to make me laugh and keep my mind preoccupied, but I couldn't get him off my mind. One day after about a week, I finally heard from him. The sound of his ringtone sent me flying over the couch trying to make it to that phone. After agonizing over missing him, hearing his voice was the sweetest melody to my ears. He asked me if I wanted to come to Providence to see him. He didn't even have to ask the question. Of course. I wanted to see him. He set up everything and it wasn't long before I was on my way to Providence to see the man who I just knew was my soul mate. From the moment I stepped foot off that Peter Pan line charter bus, I knew I had gotten myself into a situation that my butt was not ready to be in. As I explored his world that weekend, I realized just how little I knew about him. Every day we needed a different plan to simply make it through the day. He didn't have a refrigerator stock with food or even a place for us to lay our heads down that night. If we wanted to eat, we had to figure out how to make it happen. If we needed to sleep, we had to figure out a safe place. With cautious eyes, I watched as he maneuvered the streets and the people on them. I made sure I didn't miss anything so that I could preserve my safety. I didn't miss the way he got high to stay focused, yet relaxed. I watched as he sold drugs to ensure that we ate. I listened to his conversations, tuned into his lessons, and watched him like a hawk. At the end of the weekend, as I was planning to get back on the bus to return to Job Corps, Jeffery sat down next to me. I could tell by his pensive gaze that he was contemplating something. "Would you be willing to stay here with me?" he asked the question on his mind.

"Like never go back to Job Corps?" I asked for further clarification.

"Yea. Move to Providence with me," Jeffery offered. My heart responded quickly with a yes because despite his unconventional lifestyle, I loved that boy. However, my head had to take precedence over my heart. "No," I answered. As I look back on it now, I'm fully aware of how that simple yes or no decision could have completely altered the trajectory of my life. I'm proud of my younger self for having the courage to say no. I knew that I just wasn't built for that type of lifestyle. There was more in store for my life. As he dropped me off at the bus station, he was more disappointed than he was upset. I imagine because he saw my potential as an asset. I may not have yet realized my potential, but he did. I only saw Jeffery one more time after that day. It was about five years later and he had just gotten out of jail. He was still living the same life that he was five years prior. My heart hurt for him. Given a different situation and a few different choices, he could have made someone an amazing husband.

I stayed in Job Corps for another year. I met some amazing people and definitely had my share of memories and created lifelong friends, but I knew that my time there had expired. I had accomplished all that I could, but I stayed there as long as I could because I was too scared to face reality beyond Job Corps. Eventually, the Job Corps leaders terminated me from the program because they caught me and a guy sneaking in and out of each other's room. I remember heading back home on that Peter Pan bus, dreading what I was about to face. I was going to have to stay with my aunt. Even though I was grateful that she offered me a home to sleep in, the conditions weren't stable. There would be times that there was no electricity. The house had roaches that were pretty much our roommates. Since I didn't have a bed of my own, I would sleep on the floor, couch, or wherever I could find a place to lay my head. No one gave me a curfew, any guidance, and I had absolutely no support. Those ended up being some of my darkest days. One day I woke up and realized that I had enough, and I didn't have to live this life. I called my cousin Delita and asked her to get me out of there. She had her husband pick me up immediately. I packed up as much as I could in a few trash bags and never looked back. I moved back home with my adopted parents and began the process of getting my life back on track.

REFLECTIONS:
A Prodigal Child

You may be familiar with the parable in the Bible about the prodigal son. Just in case, you aren't, I'll give you an abridged version. The prodigal son wanted to leave his father's home. The father gave his son his inheritance and sent him off. While the son was away, he squandered all of his inheritance. After he had spent everything, there was a famine in the land. The son ended up feeding pigs and longing to fill himself with the pig's food because he was so hungry. The son remembered how well the servants ate in his father's household, so he went back to his father's house to be a servant. He told his father that he was no longer worthy of being his child but begged to be his servant. The father welcomed his son back as a royal part of the family, not a servant.

Jesus told this parable to show us how God will accept us back with open arms. This parable also shows us that sometimes we hit rock bottom. When God allows us to hit rock bottom, it's to warn us that we aren't in the right place. Sometimes we have to go back and start again. That's when we create space for something better.

There's a blessing in your restart. Don't miss it.

Chapter
Six

There was something about going back. Often times, we hear people say, "Keep moving forward." However, I realized that in my journey there was wisdom in going back. Back to unresolved issues, back to past hurts and pains, and back to people that had open chapters in my life. When I had to go back home to live with my parents, I went back with so much shame. I knew that my parents, specifically my father, had so many dreams for me. It was heartbreaking to look in his eyes and see the hope he had for me, knowing all the things I had done. I had gotten a taste of real life and had engaged in some behavior that caused me to be embarrassed about some of the choices that I made. Being in their presence again after leaving with my belongings in a trash bag was definitely a humbling experience. Especially, since I resurfaced carrying an identical trash bag full of my things. My mother didn't waste any time reminding me of the rules of her house. "You need to get a job," she started her checklist of demands. "You won't be running in and out of my house. I expect you to be in church every Sunday. Your chores need to be done every Saturday morning," she said, making her requests clear. I went from having no structure or rules at all, to very strict and structured household. I had forgotten what it was like. It is quite the awakening, but I committed to the process.

I found a job quickly and began working. I got up every day, walked a mile to the bus stop, and then took two buses to get to my job. I would work constantly just to avoid having to spend too much time at home. When I was home, I would stay in my room and sing. I absolutely loved to sing. Singing was an outlet for releasing my pain. During that time, I had only one boyfriend. He was only about a year older than me in age, but again, light years ahead of me in life experience. I remember he would pick me up from work every day, and if he couldn't come, he would send one of his boys to pick me up. The way he looked out for me and my safety made me feel so special. His friends would take me home so that I could change my clothes and then they would take me straight to his house. Somedays, I would be at his house by myself for hours. Other days, he would be home with me for the entire day. Eventually, that became my daily routine until one day he called me and literally called me every name in the book. My heart was broken. He told me that one of his friends said that he had slept with me. The accusation was so absurd that I thought he was playing with me at first, but he was dead serious. It made me so angry. I couldn't believe that he doubted my commitment to him. We broke up, and I was done. I changed jobs and decided to move on. Two months later, my mom kept telling me that a man had stopped by the house and each day he left roses with no card. One day, I came home from work and he was there sitting in front of my house with two dozen roses and a bouquet of balloons. He apologized for not believing me and begged me to take him back. As I looked in his face, thinking of all the names he called me, and how he literally accused me of sleeping with his friend, I decided that I would never allow a man to treat me like that again. A man would never make me so dependent on him that I would have to see myself in the reflection of his eyes in order to recognize my own face.

It seemed like just as I got yourself back on track, there was someone disguised as an angel that caused me to lose focus and fall in love. I reflect on it now and laugh because I feel so silly even thinking about how I allowed love to take me on a journey that would cause me so much heartache. One day I received a call from one of my birth cousin, Neily. She had met someone that she thought I would be compatible for me. She mentioned that she had met him through his brother and that he was such a sweet guy. I told her to give him my number and maybe we could connect. He called a few days later and introduced himself as Mike. We talked on the phone for hours, getting to know each other. He still lived with his father, but he worked a fulltime job. He told me that he had two kids but wasn't with their mother any longer. This was the first time I had ever considered dealing with someone with children, and I had no clue what I was about to get myself involved in. When he said that he lived in Bridgeport, I probably should have left him alone right then and there, but I didn't. Something about him was appealing to me, so when he asked if he could come see me, I obliged. Mike and I had planned to meet each other in person for the first time and go on our first date. When I woke up that morning, I was feeling terrible. My stomach was hurting very badly, but I wanted to meet the man I had been sharing so many conversations with over the phone. He pulled up, and the nervous butterflies in my stomach didn't help the pain that I was already feeling. My heart pounded in my chest as I watched him get out of the car and walked towards me. The closer he got to me, the better I was able to see his features. I realized that I wasn't attracted to him physically. He wasn't ugly, he just really wasn't my type. For a moment I started regretting making plans with him, but then he began to speak, I remembered why I liked him. He was very polite and told me that I looked beautiful. He had good sense of humor and made me laugh.

Mike opened the car door for me, and we drove all the way back to Bridgeport. By the time we got there, my stomach had begun hurting to the point where I couldn't even stand up. Our first date ended up being in the emergency room of Bridgeport Hospital. The crazy thing is I wasn't even embarrassed. He made me feel so comfortable and made sure that I was okay. After I was feeling better, Mike took me back home that evening and I knew that I wanted to see him again.

That night was the beginning of a more serious relationship between us. He began picking me up every weekend and then eventually, I completely stopped going back home. I moved in with him at his dad's house, and we pretty much started playing house. He would go to work and I would stay in the house. I cleaned, took care of the laundry, and whatever else needed to be done. His kids came over on the weekend and I assumed the role of stepmom. He did a pretty good job at keeping his children's mother and I separate. Her name was Marjorie, and although we weren't trying to be best friends, I thought that she was a nice person. We didn't have any major issues with each other than a little tension simply because I was the new girlfriend. What I didn't know at the time was that Marjorie and Mike had just broken up just a few months or so before Mike and I met, so there were quite a few unresolved issues between the two of them. What I also didn't know was that Mike also had another baby on the way with a different woman, named Toya. The baby with Toya was one of the main reasons why Marjorie and Mike had split up. Toya moved out of state, so it was easy for him not to tell me about her.

For the most part, our relationship was easy. I was the new girl around, so no one knew me. I stayed in the house most days while he ripped and ran the streets. If I went anywhere, it was to the corner store and back. Mike had a few sisters so there was always someone in the house to talk to or laugh with. Eventually, his crew started throwing parties at a local club. Every once and a while I would make an appearance at one of the parties, but for the mostly, I stayed in the house.

One day as Mike and I drove around, my mouth watered for a combination of beef, onions, pickles, tomato, lettuce, ketchup, and mayonnaise, all on a sesame bun. "Can I get a whopper?" I asked. I had been craving a whopper from Burger King all day. Mike took me through the Burger King drive thru and I got my sandwich. As I sat in the car, eating that whopper my craving was immediately satisfied. The satisfaction was short lived. Moment later, I started feeling queasy, and those onions, pickles, tomato, lettuce, ketchup, mayonnaise, and beef on a sesame bun came back up. My body was letting me know that something wasn't normal. The next day, I went and purchased a pregnancy test. As I waited for the results, I sat on the edge of the bed with my knee bouncing just as fast as my racing heart. I kept imaging the results coming back positive and my life never being the same. After what seemed like forever, it was finally time to look at the results. I was indeed pregnant. Sitting stiffly on the bed, I stared off into oblivion, dumbfounded. I was still putting together the pieces of my own life and trying to come to terms with growing up without my mother. Whether I was ready or not, at the age of nineteen, I was going to be someone's mother.

REFLECTIONS:

God Needs Your Help.

There comes a point in our lives when God will require us to contribute to our own life. He will give us the knowledge and the tools that we need, but it will be our job to put them to use. Because God gave us freewill—the power to choose Him or not—

He needs us to stop sitting idlily, allowing life to happen to us and become active participants in our lives.

When I learned that I was going to be a mother, it was time for me to start contributing to my destiny. If I started putting more effort into building up myself, then my son would benefit from it. If I started setting goals for myself, it became more likely for me to reach them. The thing is God doesn't need us to do much to get started. He just needs baby steps from us. Once we take a baby step, He will reveal the next step. I want to encourage you to get started. Take a small step toward God. Set a goal that will get you closer to a dream that you have. Help God help you by contributing to your life.

Chapter Seven

Pregnant. What had I gotten myself into? I was carrying a baby by a man that already had two kids and one on the way. He was barely capable of taking care of the kids that he already had, and I was going to bring another one into this situation. Abortion was never an option for me, so I focused on getting myself together and quickly. I began putting a plan in place—one that only involved me. Mike had already shown me that he wasn't a responsible father, so I mentally began to prepare myself to be a single mother. I found a part time job, created a layaway that had everything my baby would need at Walmart, and put in an application for housing with the Housing Authority. The first few months were easy. I had a ton of energy and spent my time preparing for my baby while going back and forth to my prenatal appointments. By the fourth month, my body began itching uncontrollably. The itch was intense. It seemed like no matter how much I scratched, it would never go away. Nothing could soothe it. I made an appointment with my doctor. Her ran some tests but didn't come up with a diagnosis. They prescribed various anti itch creams, but nothing worked. I realized that I was going to have to figure out how to make it through the pregnancy on my own. The fabric of my clothes had begun irritating my skin, so I began staying in the house more often, wearing minimal clothes. My doctor deemed my pregnancy as high risk. Every week I had to go into the hospital to have my blood pressure checked. The baby and I also had to have our hearts monitored. The pregnancy had begun wearing me out and I still had a ways to go.

One day Mike came home and said he needed to talk to me. He told me that he wanted to go see his daughter that was by Toya. The baby was seven months old and he hadn't met her yet. Toya and the baby were living in Texas with her grandparents, and Mike wanted to go to see her for the first time. I often think back on that day and I ask myself, "What were you thinking?" At the time I thought, of course he should go see his baby. Therefore, I told him that I thought it was a great idea. I was trying to be as supportive as possible, and I really wanted him to be able to meet his daughter. Mike went to Texas for a week. The whole time he was there, he would call and check on me and the baby, doing everything that made me feel secure. However, I found out later that he and Toya were sleeping together and apparently, he proposed to her. They had gotten so close that when Mike asked Toya if he could bring his daughter back with him for a few weeks, she said yes. The baby's birthday was coming up, so Toya allowed him to bring her up to meet his family and to see her family that still lived in Connecticut. When he came back home, I fell in love with her little chubby and smiley self instantly. Despite all of my medical issues, I took care of her as if she was my own. I changed her diapers. I fed her. I put her to sleep. Everywhere I went, she was by my side. As I took care of her and felt my baby grow within my womb, I had this sudden urge to see the woman whose womb I grew within. My mother was still in prison. One day I called my grandfather to get an update on her. He didn't have much information, so I called the prison to inquire about my mother. They told me that she was still there and that she was extremely sick. Due to her sickness, they agreed to release her. They just needed someone to release her too. I called my grandfather again, relaying the message from the prison. He agreed to allow my mother to live with him, and I would care for her. The following week, my mother was released from prison. I wasn't able to be there to see her walk out of the jail for good because I had a doctor's appointment, so my grandfather picked her up. Immediately after my appointment ended, I went to my grandfather's house to await my mother's arrival. My grandfather returned later that evening but to my surprise, my mother was not with him. "Where is she?" I asked my grandfather, confuse and a bit annoyed because I had been waiting on her.

"She wanted to go see a friend, so I dropped her off," he explained. "She's just over on the east end of Bridgeport. She'll be home later."

The next day, I went back to my grandfather's house and waited for my mother for hours, but she never showed up. I called her at the number that she gave my grandfather, but she never answered. The next day, I returned yet again, waiting for her to arrive. As I sat in that house waiting hour after hour for her to show up, my blood began to boil. The more minutes that ticked by, the hotter I felt inside. As I waited, the phone started to ring. It was my mother. "Where are you?" I yelled at her as if I was the mother.

"I'm at my friend's house," she yelled back, letting me know that she was going to do what she wanted. I answered her with another stern yell, and she reciprocated my tone. We went back and forth yelling at each other for the next few minutes before she finally just hung up on me. My throat started closing up and tears began escaping my eyes. I just sat there and cried, allowing myself to release. I couldn't understand how she could be given yet another chance to get her life in order and be a mother, but she still chose the streets over me. I felt the last little bit of hope snap inside along with me aching heart. That drug life has so much of a hold on her that it caused her to reject her own daughter. She was dying. Why wouldn't she want to spend all the time she had left getting to know me? She had already missed my entire childhood. Why didn't she seem to want me as much as I craved her? It was unbearable to think about.

After that rejection from my birth mother, it became harder for me to keep my head above water. My relationship with Mike started to fall apart. He was staying out later and later, and I was getting calls from women saying that he was cheating on me. I felt the most vulnerable that I have ever felt in life. I was preparing to bring a life into the world—the time when I needed people the most—and my boyfriend decided to cheat on me, knowing what I was going through with my mother. I was stressed out. I began losing weight and my hair had begun falling out. I was miserable and I looked it.

The following week, I went to my weekly prenatal appointment. My blood pressure was up, and I was not at all surprised. My world had been spinning out of control. When I arrived home from my weekly appointment, I noticed that I had missed a ton of calls from my cousin Neily. As I picked up the phone to call her back, I heard a car blowing its horn outside. I looked out the window to see Neily outside. I walked to the car with a smile growing into laughter because she had been blowing me up. Neily didn't even crack a smile in return. Her face remained serious, "What's up?" I asked her.

"I need to tell you something," she responded gravely. "What? My mother is dead?" I guessed with a smirk. When the words came out of my mouth, I didn't believe them. I was just talking.

"Yes," she confirmed. "And they need you to come to your grandfather's house."

I stared at her in disbelief, feeling my world crumble beneath me. There was no way she just told me that my mother had died. My mother and I still had so many conversations to have. I had so many unanswered questions for her. There were still so many unlived experiences. We never got the chance to sit around the table and laugh during a holiday meal. She would never get to look into the face of her grandchild. As I came back to myself, the realization hit me. My mother was dead. When I arrived at my grandfather's house, there was an already a group of family and friends that had gathered to reminisce about my mother. I sat down, listened as they all swapped stories and shared jokes about the firecracker that was Alexis "TuTu" Choice. I would never know the woman that they were speaking about. There wasn't any more opportunity for us to have experiences, conversations, or create memories. She was gone. I couldn't help but replay the last conversation that we had. I told her that I wished she was not my mother and now, she wasn't. I locked myself in the bathroom and cried until I felt raw inside. Maybe it was my pregnancy hormones, but I just couldn't stop crying. Suddenly, I remembered that I wasn't the only person who had lost their mother. I needed to get in contact with the prison and let my twin brother know that he had lost a parent too. My mother's siblings did all of the planning for the funeral. All I had to do was write the obituary, which was short since there wasn't much that I knew of my mother. The day of the funeral, the prison allowed my brother to come and view our mother's body before the service. I kept thinking of what he must be going through having to view the body of the women who gave us up all by himself. I wondered if he cried, if he was scared, or if he cared at all.

As I walked into the funeral, a chill entered by body as I thought about seeing my mother laying stiff in a casket. The last time I had seen her, I was fourteen and she was still seemed full of life even though she had to take pills. Forcing my feet forward, I slowly made my way up the aisle. My feet seemed so heavy as I tried to get to her. Halfway up the aisle, my knees buckled, and I got lightheaded. I dropped. My family rushed to my side, picking up my seven month pregnant self from the floor to carry me out of the funeral home. My body just wouldn't allow me to see her like that. That day, my heart hardened in a way that I had never experienced before. I was hurt, I was disappointed, and I was angry. I was slowly losing my mind and there was no one to help me.

REFLECTIONS:
When God Says No

When my mother passed away, part of me passed away too. I had been praying, groaning, crying, and begging for a chance to have a real relationship with her. God heard every one of those groans. He saw every tear. He listened to every prayer, but that wasn't God's plan for our lives. My mother's purpose was to bring me into this world. Outside of giving birth to my brother and me, she had a different path to walk and a battle of her own to overcome. I had to come to terms with the fact that her life path didn't include a relationship with me, even though I wanted it badly.

Grief is that part of life that you can't outsmart. You just have to succumb. Give yourself permission to have emotions and give yourself grace as you recalibrate.

It's not easy accepting that you are not apart of their purpose.

Chapter Eight

After my mother's funeral, I went through a process of realization. I realized that although I had an adopted family, and had met a part of my birth family, I was alone. My twin brother was in prison, my mother was dead, and I had no clue who my birth father was. I was in a toxic relationship with a man whose arms weren't large enough to hold me, but because I had no one else, I forced myself into his arms. At seven months pregnant, I was below the weight I should have been. My hair had begun falling out due to stress, and I had lost my drive. One day while cleaning up our third-floor makeshift apartment in Mike's fathers house, his father called me downstairs to his apartment. This request completely through me off guard. Although I had been living in his house going on almost a year, we rarely spoke. He wasn't mean to me, just very stern. I watched him as he worked hard and took care of all of his children. He loved hard, but he practiced tough love. You live in his house; you follow his rules. I made my way down the three flights of stairs, feeling extremely nervous as I tried to think of all the reasons why he would possibly want to speak with me. "Sit down," he said through his thick Jamaican accent. "Let me speak to you." While holding my breath, I slowly lowered into a seat at his kitchen table. I wondered if he could see the fear in my eyes as I looked at him waiting for him to speak. He took a moment to really asses me, as if he was taking inventory of my spirit. Could he see that I was desolate and broken? Was it that obvious? "What are you doing with Mike?" he asked, shaking his head.

"Huh?" I replied, confused by his question. "What do you mean? We are in a relationship. We're having a baby in a few weeks." "No," he said, shaking his head even more as if I were missing it. "What are you doing with him? Why are you with him?" Staring into his face, I took a moment to digest what he was asking me. Why was I with Mike? The only truth that I could come up with was that I was with him because I didn't have anywhere else to go. I was alone—a motherless child, a brotherless sibling. To be honest, I didn't even have myself. The conviction in his eyes pierced my soul.

"Stand up," he said. I stood up and he guided me to a nearby mirror. "Look at yourself. What do you see?" As I looked at myself in the mirror for what felt like the first time in years, I saw a face looking back at me that I didn't recognize. My skin was pale. I looked frail. My hair was broken off and damaged. The reflection of the girl staring back at me was embarrassing to look at. "How did I get here?" I whispered to myself. A warm stream of tears started down my face and I didn't stop them. I knew in that moment that I had to get my life together, and as much as I wanted a family for my unborn son, Mike could not be a part of it. I left his apartment that day determined to do better, but not sure how I would start. My life was literally in shambles. Housing had not come through yet, and I didn't have anywhere to go except for his house. Until I could figure out where to stay, I figured I needed to make the best of my current situation. I spent my days preparing for my son arrival. I kept my mind focused on bringing him into this world safely. My cholestasis had been getting worse lately. The itching was beyond unbearable, and I wasn't sure how much more I could take. I had passed out because my heart raced so badly that I would lose consciousness and have to be rushed to the emergency room a few times. After that happened two times, my doctor decided that it was best to induced me. The doctor scheduled to induce me on July 7th. I went home and got my son's crib ready. I packed my bag, and I called to set up a babysitter to watch Mike's baby girl while we were at the hospital. On the morning of July 7th, Mike took me to the hospital and then left to run errands for his older son's birthday party, which happened to be that same day. Since the doctors stated it would be quite a few hours before it would be time to push, I didn't see any point in him missing the party. After about two hours, I began to feel weak. When the nurse checked my vitals and did an ultrasound, she noticed that the baby's heart was skipping. My doctor made the decision to do an emergency C-section. I was so scared. I was not prepared to give birth via C-section. Not to mention, I was alone. I frantically began calling Mike, but his phone just rang and rang. I called his son's mothers house and she told me that he was at the store picking up the cake. My last option was to call the store and ask them to page him and let him know I was about to have the baby. They were able to find him, and he rushed to the hospital. He walked through the door just as they were preparing to roll me out the room. I can't remember what happened next because once they gave me that epidural and I was off to la la land. When I awoke, I was already in the recovery room and the nurses were calling my name. It turns out, they gave me to much epidural, and I couldn't seem to wake up. I was extremely groggy, so it was hours before I was able to hold my bundle of joy. He was born premature and only weighed five pounds. He was so light; the nurses were scared that I would drop him if they put him in my arms due to the medicine. He was absolutely beautiful. He had a head full of hair and he looked like a little Indian porcelain doll. Jamir Jaquese Hamilton was born on July 7, 2002. I was a mother now. It was my responsibility to raise my little boy into a man and nurture him. It was quite a heavy weight to accept. My first visitor was Mike's oldest sons mother. I was so surprised because although we weren't on bad terms, we didn't exactly have a relationship. However, she came to visit and brought along lots of gifts for Jamir. Her kind gesture really touched my heart, and I knew from that day on, we would be friends. She went out of her way to make sure that I knew that our children were siblings and she wanted them to have a great relationship. Unfortunately, that joy didn't last long. My next visitor was Mike's baby mother from Texas. Yup, you read it correctly. She had flown to Connecticut to pick up her daughter and thought it would be a good idea to stop by the hospital and meet me for the first time, on the day that I just gave birth. When she walked in the door, I immediately sensed her negative spirit. She didn't say anything that was rude or mean, but there was just a certain air about her that gave off an unpleasant feeling. We conversed for about fifteen minutes and then she left.

When she walked out the door, I knew that I needed to make sure I had some things in order when I left the hospital with my son. The next day I made sure that Mike signed Jamir's acknowledgment of birth paperwork and his birth certificate. I then called the child support office to figure out how I could put Mike on child support. Although we were together, I wanted to ensure that even if that changed, he was forced to financially provide for his son. I may have been young, but dumb I was not. When we left the hospital just a few days later, I had Mike take me directly to the Department of Social Services to sign all of the child support paperwork. He thought I was going to apply for food stamps, which I did, but my main purpose was to get the child support paperwork completed. After leaving the Department of Social Services, we pulled up in front of Mike's house. He seemed nervous, lingering in the car as if he didn't want to get out. He was moving slower than I was, and I was the one moving very slow simply because my body had just undergone major surgery. I felt like there was a ton of bricks sitting on my abdomen. We finally got out of the car and went inside the house. When we finally reached the third floor where our room was, something felt strange. I felt like someone had been in our room. It was a weird feeling, but I could tell something wasn't right. I began unpacking my hospital bags and getting our son settled into his new home in an attempt to take my mind off of the fact that my stomach was in knots, and it wasn't because I had just had a baby. After unpacking, I made my way downstairs to the second floor so I could watch TV and hang out with Mike's sisters. When I opened the door to the apartment, the knots in my stomach all began to make sense. Mike's babys mother from Texas was sitting in the living room with her legs crossed as if she belonged there. I looked at her and she looked back at me with entitlement. I was a bit shocked because I was under the impression that she was staying at her family's home during her visit. Mike never mentioned to me that she was at our house. As soon as she saw me, the smart comments began from her. Her main intention was to make sure I knew that her and Mike had slept together. My heart sank. After all, that I had done to take care of her and Mike's daughter, I couldn't believe that they would do that to me while I was laying up in the hospital recovering from giving birth. With all the pain that I was in, I wasn't in the mood to argue, but I did. We argued back and forth and as our voices began to escalate so did the tension. It wasn't long before we were in each other's faces, spitting out every curse word that we could think of. We called each other every name but the one our birth certificates. The closer we got in each other's faces, the more the argument ignited. The arguing turned physical, and Mike's sisters started trying to pull us apart. Their father ran upstairs cussing out both of us in his Jamaican accent, and proving to me that I had allowed his son to turn me into someone that I should be ashamed of, and I was. I was extremely ashamed of myself, but my heartbreak hurt more than my shame. I needed to get out of there and get out quickly, but I didn't have anywhere to go. I ended up going to Mike's older sisters house for a few days while I tried to get my thoughts in order. She had four children of her own in a small two-bedroom apartment, so I knew I couldn't stay there for long. Even with no place to call home for me and my son, I still found time to entertain Mike's baby mother. The heartbreaking pain had festered into anger. I refused to let Mike or his baby's mother play me like I was stupid. I would spend my days thinking of ways to torment her, baiting her, because I wanted her to feel pain like I felt pain. I wanted her to be miserable because I was feeling miserable. One day, she took the bait, telling me she was ready to settle our feud once and for all. I drove over to her family's house and stopped right out front, ready to whoop her behind. My son was in his car seat in the back, but I was too full of rage to let that stop me. In my mind, I was going to put hands on her, for the both of us. She had disrespected me and my son the moment she had walked into the hospital room after his birth. Even with all of my stitches from my c-section, I was ready to fight. Before I could get out the car, she ran up on my side door and tried to punch me in my face. With my son listening from the back seat, I grabbed his sister's mother by her hair, rolled up the window, and drove down the street. A sinical smile spread over my face as I drove along with her long hair still in my car window. She ran alongside screaming, bringing my broken heart so much joy. I realized that it was dangerous, and I knew that the joy was temporary, but boy was it joy.

REFLECTIONS:
Find Your Way Back

There are moments in life when we realize that we have allowed ourselves to move passively and aimlessly into a situation. We look around and don't understand where we are or how we arrived there. We just know that we're there, involuntarily. When I looked in that mirror and realized that I didn't recognize myself, it frightened me. I had allowed someone to consume my life. I let him rob me of my self-respect, dignity, and well-being. Not only that, I had become a bitter and petty— not the kind of woman I aspired to be at all. A bomb was ticking inside of me, waiting to explode without me realizing that it was there. I had drifted off to an unknown place and I needed to find my way back. Mike's father saw my drift and called it out. He knew that my potential was greater than what I was settling for. People who call you out candidly to remind of your potential are imperative. I am here to speak into your life the way Mike's father spoke into to mine to help you find your way back. Are you a version of yourself that you can be proud of? If not, what are you doing? What baby steps can you make today that will get you closer to the person you can smile at when you look in the mirror?

Chapter Nine

Any joy brought on by evil intentions never lasts. Despite my temporary joy, I still had to face my reality. I had a baby who was less than a month old and no stable place to call home. One day I received a call from Marjorie. She heard about my situation and she wanted to help. "I don't have a lot, but what I do have is a safe place for you and Jamir," she said. Marjorie had begun dancing at a gentleman's club, so she was gone most nights. She offered her room to Jamir and me until I figured out my next move. Her apartment wasn't huge and seven people already lived there—Marjorie and her two kids by Mike, and Marjorie's older sister and her three kids. Jamir and I would make it nine people living in the apartment. Nine people living together is a lot even for a normal household, let alone a small apartment, but we made it work. While they were gone during the day, I would make sure the house was clean and dinner was cooked. I slept in her room at night and she slept in it during the day. I often think back to those few short months and become so overwhelmed with gratitude. When I was at my lowest and needed someone, it was her who God sent to my rescue. She didn't have much to give, but she gave what she could and that was more than enough for me.

While I could have stayed at Marjorie's for as long as I needed, I knew that I was delaying the inevitable. I needed to go home. I needed my family's help. Yet again, I was going to swallow my pride and humble myself. My adopted mom had come to visit me when I was in the hospital giving birth, so I was hoping she would extend some grace and allow me and her grandson to come back home. I said a little prayer and made that dreaded phone call. To my surprise, it wasn't as hard as I expected to convince my mom to allow me to come back home. She gracefully said yes. I packed me and my baby's stuff in a bunch of trash bags and headed home. I felt ashamed and embarrassed because I felt like I should have been in a better position than I was. I looked horrible. I had never looked as bad as I did during that time in my life. I had just given birth and had lost all my baby weight plus some due to stress. I was fitting a size fourteen in kid's clothes. I almost looked unrecognizable. As much as I wished that I were moving into my own place, I honestly felt a sense of peace moving back home because I knew I would have a safe place to sleep, food to eat, and space to find myself again. As we pulled up to the house, I prepared myself mentally to fess up and own all of my mistakes. I especially had to prepare myself to look my father in the face and not be the picture of the boss daughter he always affirmed me to be. Taking a deep breath, I got out of the car and did what my newborn son needed me to do. Walking up to the door and knocking felt so strange to me. I actually felt like a stranger at a house that I had called home for much of my life. The transition wasn't hard, but it didn't come of course without rules to follow. The rules were quite different now since I was coming back as a mother, not just a daughter. I was able to move back into my old room in our finished basement. It didn't look much different from how I had left it. Some of my old teenage blow up furniture was still filled with air. The room was also surrounded by books that my dad had placed in there. I began unpacking all of Jamir's clothes and mine. What used to be my dressers, now became his dressers, filled with t-shirts, socks, tiny boy clothes, and receiving blankets. My entertainment center that held my photo albums of my friends and I, and tons of the latest CD's was now the home of diapers, wipes, and formula. I threw away the inflatable furniture that I spent all of my Ruby Tuesday paychecks on, and in its place was a baby swing and a bassinet. After I finished unpacking, I stood back and looked at the room full of baby items. That's when it really hit me in the silence of my childhood bedroom. I was a mother with a three-month-old son. Demoralizing tears began to fall from my eyes because this was not the life I had dreamed for myself. Deep down, I knew that I could do better. I had always been a smart girl. I just needed to figure out how to get it together. In the meantime, I settled into my new life, doing my best to focus on my son and his needs. Some of my older brothers' friends would come over and hang with him and whenever they came, they would take Jamir off my hands for a little while so that I could I sleep or run to the store to get refills of wipes, diapers and formula. They helped me out by playing with him in our basement living room.

Although, I was getting to a new normal, I still had to deal with the remnant of my past, which included my son's father. His baby mother had temporarily moved in and while she was there, I was invisible. He wasn't checking on our son or helping in any way. Every one of our phone conversations ended in an argument. I grew tired of his disrespect. Every chance that I got, I was heading to Bridgeport to damage his car, which was his most prized possession. I did whatever I could think of to that car. I figured if he wasn't driving it to see his son, then he didn't need to drive it anywhere. I was consumed with a man who was treating me like crap because I didn't know how to love myself. There were many days when I would stay in my room in the dark, falling into a deep depression. My mother had to start taking my son to her room so that he wouldn't be subject to my darkness. I would cry for hours, allowing myself to be a bitter victim. I somehow allowed myself to believe that if he didn't want to be with me, no one would, unable to see my own worth and value. I wasted so much time focusing on what I was not, and spent zero time actually trying figure out who I truly was. At that time in my life, I was a mother and I had a son that required my attention. I couldn't give it to him.

"Sana, when are you going to remember who you are?" my brother's friend Jamel asked me one day while we were sitting in the living room watching TV. He had Jamir in his arms and asked me that question out of nowhere. His question riddled me. I looked at him with blank eyes. "Remember back in school when you had so many dreams? You never let people disrespect you, and you always had a smile on your face," he went on. I sat there and allowed his question to take up space. I never answered him. I silently made a promise to myself that one day I would reintroduce that woman to him again.

After a few months of being back home, and me stalking the housing authority daily, I finally received a call from them letting me know that they had an apartment available for me if I wanted it. I eagerly accepted it, but when I found out it was in Marina Village, my heart sank just a bit. Nevertheless, I was ready for a fresh start for my son and I. This was an opportunity to finally have something to call my own.

REFLECTIONS:

Not Alone

When is the last time you've taken inventory of your life? Like really sat down to look at each area of your life to see what's bearing good fruit and what parts are toxic and rotten? It's necessary to take inventory every now and again of your relationship, friendships, and family ties.

Everything around me kept alerting that my relationship wasn't bearing good fruit. Even my boyfriend's very own father sat me down and told me that I could do better than his son. However, I kept holding on to that toxic fruit until it splattered in my face. God will let stuff splatter in your face, especially when we don't listen. Because I didn't listen, God had to remove me from that situation the hard way. I ended up couch surfacing with my newborn baby. Thankfully, God's grace was sufficient for me. He sent me an unlikely friend in Marjorie. That is exactly how God works. He will never pull you out of something and not give you something in its place to sustain you. God was there for me the whole time even though I didn't realize it, and He is there for you too. So, when you're going through a difficult journey, know that you aren't going through it alone.

God's replacement will always be better thatn what you lost.

Chapter
Ten

Marina Village is a housing project located in Bridgeport, Connecticut. Marina Village was built in 1940 and was run by the Bridgeport Housing Authority. It was one of the worst housing projects in Bridgeport, known for drugs, murders, and gang activity. When I received the news that I was getting an apartment in Marina Village, I wasn't thinking about the drugs, murders or gangs. I was just so happy to have the opportunity to have my own apartment for the first time. My plan was to mind my business and take care of my son, nothing more, and nothing less.

When I received the keys to my tiny apartment located at twenty Ridge Road, I felt like I had finally accomplished something that was going to be good for my son and me. I walked through that place envisioning a color scheme, picture frames, throw pillows and all. I was determined to make that place a home for my budding family. I went to Walmart and finally paid off the balance for my layaway that I had started months in advance in preparation for my first apartment. Marjorie's mother was moving down south, so she gave me her old living room set. I went to a popular furniture place on Boston Avenue and was able to purchase a bedroom set for my room. Finally, I got Jamir's crib from his grandfather's house and put it up in his own room. By the time I moved everything in and put it in its place, I felt a sense of peace for the first time. I remember my mom always used to tell me that you don't have to act like where you came from. That was my mindset as I created a safe place within the four walls of my home. There may be shootings and drugs outside my door, but on the other side there would be love, peace, and comfort.

After I moved back to Bridgeport and now had my own place, Mike suddenly wanted to get back together. I knew in my heart that he believed that he loved me, but he certainly did not treat me the way I deserved to be treated. My head and heart battled because I believed that I loved him too. However, in my head I saw my better judgement giving me the side eye, letting me know that I could do much better. Despite all of that, I chose to follow my heart instead of my head. That heart will have you all messed up, making life-altering decisions just because it feels good. We agreed to get back together and he immediately moved in with me. Mike's best friend CL moved in with us too. He was Jamir's godfather, which was one of the best choices that Mike had ever made for Jamir and I. CL and Jamir's other godfather literally took turns filling in the empty pieces of fatherhood that Jamir experienced during the first years of his life. Although they were considered young in age, they embodied wisdom beyond their years. They gave me hope that Jamir would be okay, because they wouldn't allow him not to be. It was no surprise that when I moved into Marina, CL moved in as well. When Mike wasn't present or reliable, CL made sure that Jamir had a babysitter if I had to work second shift so that I could attend school during the day.

The first few months were easy because Mike and I were still living our own version of the honeymoon phase even though we weren't married. We didn't argue. Our communication was good. We spent quality time together. We did all the things that make you feel like you have a happy family. For me it was just something special about the feeling of having my own family, period. I would cook dinner every day and we would actually sit at the table and eat together. We would lay in the bed on a rainy Saturday and watch TV. It was just easy and beautiful for a while until Mike's old patterns started emerging just when I least expected it. He started hanging out later and later, not answering his phone when I called. This type of activity became a trigger for me. I hadn't forgotten about all the times he cheated on me and all the drama we went through only a year or so prior. This time the difference was that I was in an apartment that only had me and my son's name on the lease. I could make him leave at any point and I did. After that, we went through a phase where we constantly broke up and then got back together. Eventually, I got tired of it.

There was a little store located within the project. It was right at the end of my street and if you sat on the front stoop, you could see the store easily. When we first moved in, I avoided going to that store. I didn't want to walk through the sea of men that seemed to always be standing in front of the store or on the side gambling. Sometimes they would just stand there and have deep conversations. Nevertheless, they were always standing out front, so I didn't go, but when Mike began to resume his usual cheating tendencies, things changed. I figured I would start making him jealous. Sis had started to gain some weight, and I am talking about that good weight in all of the right places after I had my son and decreasing my stress. You can say that I was feeling myself a bit. I put on a cute outfit strutted to the store, past the sea of men. I had my one-year-old son with me and we went in and bought something random. Afterall, I wasn't at the store to buy anything. I was there to make Mike jealous. Going into the store became me and Jamir's daily routine. Every time that we would walk in, I would get a few men that would try to shoot their shot. I never engaged, but it felt good to have someone pay attention to me again. It was a reminder that I still had it. I no longer wondered if anybody other than Mike would want me, and honestly, it made me feel good. While at the store one day, I got to the register to pay for our items and the clerk told me that it was already taken care of. I looked around the store to see who paid the bill for me, but there was no one else in the store. When I asked who paid for my stuff, the store clerk insisted that he didn't know who paid it. He just knew that a man paid it. This went on for a few visits. Every time I went to pay, it was already paid for. I knew by this time that I had an admirer, but I had no idea who it could be. It wouldn't be long before he revealed, his identity and my life as well as those who I love would be at risk. What I had not anticipated, was that along with him would come days where he would want to sit in the house with his friends and chill or sit on the stoop with his friends and chill.

REFLECTIONS:

The Desires of Your Deceitful Heart

I'm sure all parents can relate to telling their kids not to do something, but they do it anyway. It can be a small thing like telling them not to stand on the edge of something to prevent them from falling. Somehow, their little foot finds its way to the edge again. You might warn them a second time and then snatch them up the third time. However, if they're on that edge again, you might just let them fall, knowing they might get hurt a little bit but learn a valuable lesson at the same time. That's the kind of parent God is. He may give you the desires of your deceitful heart so that you can learn a lesson the hard way. If you keep doing the same thing repeatedly, knowing that it's wrong, God may give you what you desire and let you fall.

Chapter Eleven

Y ou know you are absolutely beautiful right?" I heard a voice say from behind me. I used one hand to put my stuff on the counter, and the other hand to struggle with Jamir as he tried to run out the door. When I finally had a good grip on my son's hand, I turned around to see the face behind the voice. My eyes locked with a man that looked to be at least a few years older than me. He had slanted brown eyes, and a beautiful smile. I just looked at him wondering who he was. I had never seen his face before. He must have seen the confusion in my expression. "Yeah, I'm talking to you," he said, making it plain for me.

"Oh. Thank you," I replied, bashfully.

"My name is Drew," he introduced himself. "What up?"

"My name is Sana," I informed him.

"I know who you are," Drew replied with confidence.

I looked at him like he was crazy. "Ummm, how do you know me?" I asked, sure that he didn't know me at all.

"I know everyone that lives out here," he said. Those words immediately made me a little nervous. I looked toward the door with the intention of leaving the items on the counter and getting out of there quickly, but when I looked at the door, I noticed for the first time that there was another man blocking anyone else from entering. I turned my attention back to Drew and tried to mask my fear. I had heard of the gang members that called Marina Village home and I was sure that I had come face to face with one of them. All types of thoughts began running through my mind as I picked Jamir up and placed him on my hip. "Don't be scared," he said in a calm voice. "I just wanted to introduce myself to you, so you can put a face to the man who has been paying for your stuff the last few weeks." It finally dawned on me. He was my admirer. My heart slowed down just a bit.

"Oh, thank for doing that," I said. "Why did you pay for my stuff?" I went on to ask him.

"Because you're a beautiful woman and I just wanted to do something nice for you. Every time I see you walk down here, you never come with your man. I know you have one because I have seen him on your stoop a few times but he always lets you walk down here through all these men by yourself." I had never taken the time to consider why Mike didn't have anything to say about me walking to the store, but Drew was right. I remained silent because I honestly didn't know what to say. "Let me get your number," he asked boldly. "I would like to call you sometimes." I hesitated. I wanted to make Mike jealous, but I wasn't trying to cheat. Before I knew it, Drew had grabbed my phone, dialed a few numbers, and his phone rang. "Don't worry about it. I got it." He handed me back my phone, paid for my stuff at the counter, threw me smile, and then was gone. Anxiously, I grabbed my bag and walked out the store. Nervous sweat beaded on my forehead as I emerged from the store. I could just feel the stares of the men as I walked by. This time they were silent instead of their usual catcalls, yoooo shorty comments, and what up. They simply gave me a head nod like it was a sign of respect and continued with their dice game. On my way home, my phone sounded with a text alert.

Make sure you lock me in – Drew. A huge smile found its way to my lips after I read his text, enhancing my walk back to my apartment.

Over the next few weeks, Drew and I played cat and mouse. Periodically, we would meet up somewhere outside of the project and just talk. We never had sex, we just talked, which honestly threw me off. Although I enjoyed speaking with him, I was always waiting for him to expect more of me, but he never did. He said he just wanted to make sure I was taken care of. Now to me, this was huge because the man I was sleeping with every night wasn't even doing that. Every time we met up, he would make sure he put money in my hand before we departed ways. One evening I received a 911 text from him. He told me to meet him behind a certain building that was abandoned. I made a quick excuse to Mike to leave the house for a few minutes and made my way the building. When I arrived, Drew seemed very fidgety. He started telling me that I needed to be more careful. It seemed that my house had become the topic within Marina. They saw many different people hanging outside, going in and out and various domestic cars always parked in front. I explained to him that those people were Mike's friends and the domestic cars were because my son's godfather worked for a car service company. "All I know, is that you need to be careful and tell them to stop being all in your house," he said. As we went our separate ways, I kept hearing his words in my ear. Something about the look in his eyes and the serious tone in his voice didn't feel right in my spirit. My gut was screaming at me to pay attention, but I pushed it to the back of my mind and eventually forgot about it.

When I was a child, I remember how my mother would walk the house around midnight, after everyone was in their beds. She would peek in each of our rooms and check the locks on the door. She did this every night for as long as I can remember. She was still doing it when I moved back home with Jamir for those few months. From my room, I could hear the pitter patter of her feet as she walked throughout the house, completing her safety check. Of course, when I moved into my own place, I implemented this routine into my own tradition. Every night between midnight and two o' clock in the morning, I would get up and do a safety check. One night, as I tip toed up the stairs, going back to my room after completing my safety check; I thought I heard a sound. Turning around, I tip toed back down the steps, carefully and intently scanning over the house. As I got closer to my back door, I could hear voices. Moving quickly, I sprinted up the steps and got into my bed. With my heart booming through my chest so loudly that I could hear it through my ringing ears, I began to pray. In the middle of my prayer, I began to hear footsteps coming up the stairs. Paralyzed with fear, my body stiffly lay unmoving until the light in my room turned on and loud voices yelled to get the f*** out of the bed. Three masked men came rushing onto my bedroom. I jumped up and began to shake Mike who was sound asleep, and snoring in the bed next to me. Before I could awake him, one of the masked men smacked him in the head with the end of a gun. He hit him with the gun repeatedly until blood gushing from Mike's head. After he seen that Mike was too injured to put up a fight, the gunman dragged him out of the bed and forced him into Jamir's room where CL was asleep. "Give me the money and drugs!" the man demanded. He was talking to CL.

"I don't have anything, I swear," CL tried telling him.

I heard the man hit CL with his gun the same way he did Mike, followed by the sound of CL's whimper as he repeatedly tried to convince him that he didn't have any drugs. Eventually the man stopped asking and just beat CL using the end of his gun. Meanwhile, in my room one of the men forced me to remove my clothes. He stood over me, unzipped his pants, preparing to force himself onto me. All of a sudden, I heard a voice yell, "Yo, what are you doing? You heard him say don't hurt her." The man who was standing over me zipped his pants back into place and said, "B**** you lucky this time." The man who saved me from being raped pulled me up off the bed, walked me into my son's room and proceeded to tie me, Mike and CL up. He covered our mouths with tape, and then ran out the room, and down the stairs. I could hear them breaking dishes, and things hitting the floor as they rummaged through my home. As I sat there tied up, a sense of peace come over me, dissipating my fear. Instead of being scared, my mind began to devise a plan to get free. Wiggling my mouth from side to side and licking my lips, I was able to loosen the tape up just enough to whisper. I called CL's name and then Mike's name to make sure they weren't dead. They both responded, but CL's voice sounded very faint. "Stay with me CL," I repeated repeatedly. After about ten minutes, it got quiet downstairs. I began freeing myself from the rope, and then I freed CL and Mike. I slowly jumped up, felt around the dark room until I found my car keys. Mike helped CL get up and together we slowly went down the stairs. When we got to the front door, we ran as fast as we could to the car, jumped in, and drove to the closest hospital. It wasn't until we pulled up to the emergency room that I realized I didn't have any shoes on my feet. After getting Mike and CL checked in, I dropped my head into my hands, exhaled out a breath and started weeping. We had almost lost our lives.

REFLECTION:
The End of Me

There's a saying in the military that there is no such thing as an atheist in a foxhole. What that means is when people face near death situations, they all seek God. Even those who claim to not believe, and who are denying His power and providence over their lives. For me, facing death brought me to the end of myself. When you get to the end of yourself that means, you've ran out of options. You are relinquishing control because you realize that you aren't in control and have never been. Reaching the end of yourself is you trusting God enough to mold your life into what He wants it to be. Once that happens, God can begin His work on you.

Chapter Twelve

I stayed up all night making sure that Mike and CL were okay. Mike was discharged a few hours later, but CL was admitted and had to stay in the hospital for a couple of days. The next morning, I made my way back to my apartment. The housing authority had already called the police after seeing that my back door had been kicked in. They had the forensic police there dusting for fingerprints and interviewing the neighbors. When I arrived, they were quite surprised as they thought I had been kidnapped based on the condition of the house. They immediately began asking me questions about what happened. I told them that they all had on masks, so I couldn't see their faces. Unfortunately, I didn't have much information to provide. When I entered my apartment, the mess around the place shocked me. Everything in my kitchen and living room was tossed all over the place. There was flour, and sugar all over the floor and I could see footprints within the substances. Clearly, they were searching for drugs and must have thought it was hidden in the flour and sugar. As I made my way up the stairs, there was a trail of blood that must have been left as we ran down the stairs to escape. The bedrooms also had large amounts of blood and the rope and tape used to restrain us was still on Jamir's bedroom floor. As I stood there, I broke down in tears. The memories of last night began to flood my mind—the man hitting Mike in his sleep, the man standing over me unzipping his pants, CL's faint voice. My thoughts were interrupted by the sound of the police calling my name. They were wrapping up and wanted to let me know that maintenance men would be coming by to board up the back door which was currently leaning up against the kitchen wall. The robbers had indeed kicked it in, and that was the sound that I had heard heading back up the stairs just a few hours before. I ended up moving into a hotel for the next two weeks as I tried to figure out my next move and while CL recuperated. I knew there was no way that I could sleep in that apartment, again so I made the decision to move back to Middletown and stay with my parents. I would have been naïve to think that the robbery was a mistake. It was a wakeup call from God. My life could not keep up on this path. One day while

I was making one of my daily trips to pack up the apartment to gather my belongings, I sat on the front stoop to take a break. It was super quiet in Marina Village that day because everyone was at the infamous Freddy Fixer Parade in New Haven, Connecticut. The Freddy Fixer is nationally recognized as one of the oldest Black American parades in the northeast. While sitting on that stoop, taking my break, I saw a man walk by two times. When he walked by the first time, he lifted his chin, giving me a head nod followed by a quick, "What up Ma?" The third time he walked by, he stopped to talk to me. "What you doing?" he asked. "Just packing up my things because I'm moving out of here," I told him. He took a seat next to me on the stoop and we began talking about how quiet and hot it was outside. As he continued to talk, I realized that I recognized his voice. I had never met him or even seen him around before, but his voice was very familiar to me. "Would you like something to drink?" I offered.

"Yea, I'll take something," he said. I got up and walked into the kitchen. As I grabbed him a soda from the fridge, I kept racking my brain, trying to remember why his voice sounded so familiar to me. Suddenly, it hit me. He was one of the masked men who robbed my home. Carrying his soda, I walked back outside with a strange calm. I sat on the stoop and handed him the soda.

"Thank you," he said, taking a few sips. "Aight ma," he said as he got up to leave. "Thanks again for the drink."

I looked him square in his face and said, "No, thank you." Our eyes locked and the moment became uncomfortable. He fidgeted a bit and then started walking away. His voice was the voice of the man that stopped his partner from raping me during the robbery. As angry as I was that he was one of the men that had broken into my home, I was more thankful that he was there to stop me from being raped. I finished packing the items that I would take with me, locked up the house, and never went back.

After the robbery, I spiraled out of control. I went through so many emotions but never talked about them with anyone or reconciled what I was feeling. No one ever asked me about what took place that night or how it made me feel. Everything was bottled up within me without an outlet. I started living my life as if there was no tomorrow, because I knew firsthand what it felt like to stare death in the face. I completely broke up with Mike and only spoke with him when it had something to do with Jamir. Most times, the conversations started with disrespect and ended in an argument, so most days I wouldn't even answer his phone calls. As I settled back in at my parents' home, I was able to get a job and enroll Jamir in preschool as he was going on two years old.

I started going to clubs in Hartford every weekend. While in the club, I was introduced to ecstasy pills. Although I never smoked weed and rarely drank more than a wine cooler, ecstasy, became my drug of choice. Whenever I was on ecstasy, I was able to forget about my reality. I started doing thong contest at various clubs around the state, and eventually promoters started paying me to come out and get the crowd hyped. I was clubbing Thursday - Sunday, every single week. My father was my in-house babysitter. I would put Jamir down to bed and head out the door. My dad always watched TV down in the basement living room where my room was, so I never had to worry about someone keeping an eye on him. This was my life for the next year. I felt more lost than I ever had before and I was losing all sense of self-control. Even though I was hanging on by a thread, I was still showing up to work every day and balancing my day-to-day responsibilities. No one in my family ever realized that I was doing thong contests and taking hard-core drugs. One weekend I decided to try a new pill. The regular pills weren't giving me the high that I was looking for anymore. I was introduced to a stronger version of ecstasy called the Blue Pill. I took that pill and the next day I couldn't remember a thing that had happened the night before. When I woke up, I felt like I was having an out of body experience. My entire body felt tingly and I started hallucinating. I was scared to leave the house, so I stayed in my room for almost a week. I felt so sick, and I was vomiting constantly. It felt like it took forever to come down from that high. That's when I knew I had had enough. I wasn't ready for that life at all. I vowed to never take another drug again after that, and I never did.

I spent the next few months working hard to be a better Sana for myself and my son. I completely quit the party girl lifestyle. I got a job as a medical receptionist at a large medical group in New Britain and started looking for my own apartment. Everything was starting to look up for me. Every time things started going well, it seemed like Mike wasn't too far away, waiting to be an issue.

REFLECTIONS:
Change Me

Most of my praying had a focus on God changing my circumstances. I wanted a better man, a place to stay, and more money to help me provide. However, most times, God isn't interested in changing our circumstances. He's interested in changing us. God's work begins in our minds. He needs our thoughts to become more positive and focused on kingdom matters. We can be so consumed with praying for things that will bring us comfort, instead of the things that will build our faith, increase our wisdom, and heal our souls. The best thing that we can let God do for us is to change is from the inside out.

God wants us to be transformed from the inside out.

Chapter
Thirteen

Since I had moved back home, there was very few times when Mike came to see Jamir. If I didn't drive to Bridgeport, he would have never seen him. Therefore, I was quite surprised when he called me one Friday to say he was coming to pick up Jamir to stay the night with him. The next day, I got Jamir packed and ready to spend the weekend with his dad. I told Mike to meet me at my cousin Delita's house, since Jamir and I were already there for the weekend. When he pulled up, I notice that he wasn't alone. There was a female in the front seat of his car. The pieces began to connect together for me. Mike had called me, requesting to pick up our son, which was something that was out of character for him, just so he could get under my skin. Although we weren't together anymore, he never mentioned that he was dating someone else, nor did he ask me if I was comfortable with our son being around a woman whom I never met. I could feel my blood begin to boil. Mike should have told me that he was planning to have a woman around our son so I could have told him that I was not okay with my son being around a woman that I didn't know. "We need to talk," I said when he stepped out of the car. We walked a few feet away from the car in an attempt to have a private conversation. "Who is the woman in the front seat?" I asked candidly, not in the mood for his games. "None of your business," he replied rudely.

I cocked back my head, feeling beyond fed up with always arguing with him. "Jamir will not be going with you until it becomes my business."

He responded by to calling me a b**ch followed by about five other curse words. "You're not gonna stop me from taking my son," he said, grabbing up Jamir and taking off to his car. I ran after him. By the time I reached the car, Jamir was already in his back seat and he was behind the wheel. I jumped into the back seat and snatched the thick gold chain that he had around his neck in an effort to stop him. As I pulled that chain tightly, his head strained against the headrest. I realized that I was choking him with the chain. I pulled it tighter, blacking out in the process. I don't remember much after that except for looking at Jamir and telling him that it was going to be okay. I felt the anger that I had been holding on to for the last three years rushing to my memory. I remembered getting the phone calls from other women, letting me know that they were sleeping with the same man that I was sleeping with. I pulled tighter. I remembered hearing Mike calling me every insult as if I was nothing. I pulled tighter. I remembered how he slept with Toya while I was in the hospital recovering from birthing his baby. I pulled tighter. My thoughts were interrupted by the sound of Delita's voice. "Let him go," she screamed hysterically. The panic in her voice got through to me. I loosened my grip on the chain and heard the sound of him gasping for air. Delita pulled open the door and her husband pried my hands from the chain. Once loose, Delita's husband snatched me out of the car and carried me to the driveway. I was still fighting to get back to my son. I was able to break away from him and grab a brick. As Mike drove off with Jamir in the back seat, I hurled the brick at his car, just missing it by inches. It wasn't until I walked in the kitchen that I realized my palms were cut open and there was blood dripping from them. I had pulled the chain so hard, it cut through my skin.

As Delita cleaned up my hands and bandaged them up, she began lecturing me. "You are crazy!" she yelled. "You could have gone to prison." I just sat there in shame and tears. My body was shaking so badly that I could barely get a word out, so I just listened. I knew everything that she was saying was true. I didn't recognize myself. My own anger had scared me. That night I laid on Delita's living room couch and began speaking to God. I always turned to Him when my life was spinning out of control, but this time was different. This time I didn't want to just ask for His help and then do it on my own, I wanted Him to fix me completely. "I'm tired God," I cried out, tears heavily dripping down and soaking my shirt. "Can you just send me a man that will love me, and treat me with respect? I'm tired of being used and abused like I'm nothing." After pleading with my Heavenly Father, I closed my eyes and drifted off asleep, exhausted and drained.

The next morning, Delita woke me up, shaking me and telling me to get up. As I sat up, I was met with a huge headache. I looked at her, wondering why she was waking me up so early in the morning on the weekend. "I want you to come to church with us this morning," she said to me. I looked at her like she was crazy. Flipping my palms forward, I reminded of my bandaged hands. Not to mention, I felt the puffiness in my face, from crying myself to sleep. "There is no way I am walking into a church looking like this," I responded. Growing up, I remembered attending church. The women wore their perfectly pressed dresses with matching heels. The men had on tailored suits with matching handkerchiefs. In my mind, people never show up to church until they had it all together. They didn't show us at church with bandaged hands after choking out the father of their child. I definitely didn't feel like I had it together enough to walk into a church. I didn't want to anyone judging me. "If you just come this one time, I won't ask you again," Delita said, not giving up. We went back and forth on the subject until I finally agreed to go. I found the most appropriate looking outfit, got showered, and then dressed. When we pulled up to the church, sudden nervousness began wreaking havoc in my stomach. It had been so long since I last stepped inside of a church. I didn't know what to expect. The church was huge with a ton of cars parked in the parking lot. As I walked up the walkway, I noticed this tall, dark skinned young man sitting on the railing. He was talking on his cell phone. As I walked by, admiring his fineness, I heard a still, small, voice tell me that he was my husband. I looked at my cousin and relayed the message to her. "That's my husband," I announced confidently. She looked at me with her brows pulled together and her lips pursed. "Girl, you need to get your life together. You are here for God not no man," she said, I laughed, knowing that she was correct, but still, the man was fine and I knew what I heard. All through the service, I kept my eyes on of him. He was the drummer. I fixated on those drums, mesmerized by how good he looked playing those sticks.

Before I knew it, the preacher was headed back to his seat and I hadn't heard one word of the message. "At this time, we are going to have Josh come to the pulpit with a few announcements," the lady in the pulpit said. The fine brother from the drums stood up and hopped to the mic. This was the first time I realized that he was on crutches and that his name was Josh. He began asking for dessert donations from the ladies of the congregation. The desserts were for his father who was getting married and having a bachelor party. Then it dawned on me, his father was the Pastor. Lord, I almost fell out the pew. I MUST have heard that still, small voice incorrectly, because there was no way God would be orchestrating for the Pastor's son to be my husband. Pastor's son or not, I couldn't get him off my radar. I had already started plotting on how to get his number.

When church ended, and my cousin and her husband were talking to various people. I hung back by myself, keeping my eyes on Josh. Several people were walking up and talking to him. I waited patiently, but I was determined to get to him. Finally, Josh was alone standing by the door. I walked up to him, smiling my wide smile. "I can bake a cheesecake for the bachelor party," I offered. I had never baked a cheesecake in my life, or a cookie for that matter. I figured I could get my mom to make a cheesecake for me. That detail was insignificant, though; what was significant was that I was talking to him. I spent the entire service looking at him and imaging him as my husband, and now I was offering to bake him a cheesecake. We went back and forth with small talk for a second and then I went in for the kill. "So, can I get your number?" I asked, forwardly. He raised his eyebrow, taken aback. He wasn't expecting that question to fly out of my mouth.

"Nah, I don't give my number to ladies I meet in church," he responded in a true pastor's son fashion.

"Oh no problem," I said, waving off his concern. I called my cousin's husband, Ahmad over and then turned back to Josh. "You can give your number to my cousin's husband. He is a man. And then he can give it to me." Josh looked at me and chuckled, but he gave his number to Ahmad, and Ahmad gave it to me. I had never been happier to have had gone to church than that day. I walked out the church doors with a Kool-Aid smile on my face.

REFLECTIONS:
Growing Season

The spring season is the rainiest season, but it's the most productive season. We need the rain. Without it, nothing will grow. Likewise, in life. When it's seems to be raining nonstop in your world, rest assured that growth is coming. My life seemed like one very long season of rain, until one day it suddenly stopped raining and I started growing. Although, I was elated when the rain finally subsided, I was grateful for that season of my life because of the breakthroughs and miracles that would happen years later but trace back to that rainy season.

Chapter Fourteen

I went home that day and agonized over how long I should wait to call Josh. I decided I wasn't waiting. I picked up the phone and dialed his number. I strategically let it ring two good times and then hung up. Seconds later, he did exactly what I expected him to do. He called back. "Hello?" I answered the phone innocently as if I hadn't just called him.

"Did someone just call me from this number?" he inquired.

"Yup, I did," I responded in my most coy voice. "Do you know who this is?"

"Of course, I know. I don't give my number out to a lot of women at church," he said.

We talked for a few more minutes before he said that he would call me back. True to his word, that evening he called back. We talked for a few hours about everything under the sun, and then he asked me out on a date for that next Friday.

My cousin ended up going into labor that Thursday. She asked if I would stay at her house and watch her kids while she and Ahmad were in the hospital. I watched the kids for her, but Ahmad came home Friday evening to keep the kids while I went on my date. Josh and I decided to go to the restaurant, Fridays for our date. When we sat down at the table, we began talking, asking each other's questions and getting to know each other better. At some point, he asked me what I was looking for in a man. Pulling my shoulders back and sitting up straight, I looked him straight in his eyes and answered his question. "I don't need a man to take care of me, open doors for me, pull out my chair, spend his money on me or buy me gifts."

"Well what do you need a man for?" he asked, returning my straightforward gaze. We both busted out laughing, but I felt like an idiot. I had answered his question out of brokenness. It was the response of a woman who had not been treated right by a man, and had built up a wall for any potential suitors. Josh and I ended up back at Delita's house and stayed up all night talking until we fell asleep on the couch in the wee hours of the morning. The next morning, he got up and went to his father's wedding. After the wedding, he came right back to Delita's to spend more time with me. That same weekend, I was able to pick up the keys to my new apartment, and Josh moved in with me. When I got the apartment, it was a mess. The amenities were outdated and deteriorated. The place definitely needed updating. It was the only thing that I could afford, which wasn't much. The only furniture that I could buy with my little money was a blow-up bed for Jamir and I to share. One day while I was at work, Josh went to his own house that he shared with his two older siblings and took apart his bed to set it up in my apartment so that I would have a place to sleep.

By the time Christmas came around, we had been dating and living together for almost three months. On Christmas day, he asked me to go with him to his grandmother's house in New Haven, Connecticut. His grandmother was important to him because she raised Josh and his siblings after his mother passed away from breast cancer when he was sixteen years old. This would be the first time that I would meet his grandmother, and I was so nervous. When we knocked on the door, an older, dark skinned women, with beautiful, silver hair greeted us with a warm smile and a bubbly hello. "Nana, this is my girlfriend Sana," Josh introduced.

"Sana," she said my name thoughtfully. "Sana, I know you," she claimed, surprising both Josh and I.

Josh immediately started shaking his head. "This is the first time I'm bringing her to meet you," he said quickly, hoping his Nana hadn't mistaken me for another woman.

"No. I know her," she said adamantly. "Hold on, I'll be right back." She turned quickly and went to the back of the house. As we settled into the living room, she resurfaced just a few minutes later. She was holding a photo in her hand. She turned it toward us so that we could see that it was a picture of me. "I knew I knew you," she said, handing over the wallet-sized picture of a little girl. The little girl in the picture was me. I was five-years-old. I had three ponytails in my hair with blue barrettes on the end. My blue barrettes matched my blue outfit. I had a wide smile on my face, which brought tears to my eyes as I reflected on the things that little girl in the photo had endured. Five-year-old Sana had been physically and sexually abused to the point of hospitalization. She was taken away from her birth family and moved around, while living with strangers. That little girl had visited her mother in a prison. Young Sana had been resilient enough to make it to that couch that I was sitting on to reflect back on my life. I flipped over the picture read the back. It said: To Bishop and Sis. Powell. I must have looked at her with quite the confused face, because she quickly explained that she and her late husband was the Pastor and First Lady that shared a space with my foster parents, the Morgan's in their first building years ago. I then turned my confused face to Josh. I was shocked. Never had I expected this, and it turned out to be the best Christmas I had ever had.

Josh and I dated for the next six months, and it was a whirlwind. I fell in love with him quickly, and he became my best friend. He respected me. He always acknowledged my wisdom and life experiences, but he never made me feel ashamed because of them. He kept me laughing to the point where it brought tears to my eyes, not tears of pain like previous men, but tears of joy. I had never experienced the kind of love that I felt with Josh. We started having conversations regarding marriage. I was always firm with him that I didn't want to be anybody's live-in-girlfriend again. I desired to be a wife. I talked about it so much that he finally said, "Won't nobody MAKE me get married. I don't care if you get pregnant with my baby. I am not asking any woman to be my wife until I am ready."

On July 4, 2007, we were headed to our church for a Fourth of July church picnic. There was a song by Dave Hollister that Josh played in the car. The words talked about becoming husband and wife and I remember saying to him, "Okay, I get it. You're not going to marry me. Please turn this song off then." But he wouldn't turn off the song, he just laughed.

During the cookout, I was helping set up, and Josh's stepmother kept saying, "Be careful Sana, you don't want to spill anything on your white skirt." Then I noticed that my mom and dad pulled up. Josh's grandmother arrived also along with his two younger siblings. When I saw them, I paused for a second thinking it was strange for them to be at the picnic because they didn't attend our church. I brushed it off, assuming that Josh's parents invited them. I began noticing that Josh was acting weird. He avoided talking to me, but I brushed it off again. It began raining out of nowhere and the cookout was moved inside of the church. Everyone was sitting inside when Ahmad started singing "Love" by Musiq Soulchild. I thought the song of choice was weird for a church picnic, but then josh grabbed my hand, guided me to the front, and started professing his love for me. Before I knew it, he was on one knee. It finally dawned on me what was going on. I was so in shock that I actually tried to walk out slowly, but then I began crying and shaking. Josh asked me to be his wife and I responded with an absolute yes. It was the greatest day of my life. I still remember the calming whisper from God when He told me that Josh would be my husband.

My life has been one of a kind. One that at many times, I asked God to remove me from. I have had to overcome much pain but I have come out on the other side wounded, but not scarred. I am a true picture of God's grace and mercy. He had a plan for me before I was even formed within my mother's womb. I have deviated from that plan on many occasions as I made decisions from my flesh, but he has always kept his hand on my life and stayed right by my side. This is only the beginning of my story, and there is so much more to unfold, but if you gained nothing else from the pages of this story, please know, that the God I serve is real, and I have a story that will make you believe in Him.

REFLECTIONS:
Healer

Nothing God does or allows is an accident. Remember when I said that God is strategic and that His plans are perfectly orchestrated. God had a purpose for my life all along. Every dark moment was God constructing my testimony. I didn't know it at the time, but I would tell my story in front of many and do it unashamed and healed. I would talk about being molested and women would share for the first time that they were molested too. God had a plan to use all of my trials and resiliency to help me heal others who have gone through similar circumstances.

On my adoption day, I remember the judge asking me if I wanted to change my name. I considered changing my entire name but settled on keeping the name Sana because I couldn't imagine being called anything else. I'm so glad I kept my name because I later found out that the name Sana means healer.

From the very moment God formed me in my mother's womb, he placed an undeniable purpose on my life. All the evidence is clear, and nothing was a coincidence.

About the Author

Sana has also been featured in numerous media outlets including *Sheen Magazine, EntrepreneuHER Magazine, Voyage Dallas*, as well as on *Moments of Joy Podcast, AOL.com*, and *TBN's, the 700 Club.*

Sana Latrease is the wife to Joshua E. Cotten and the mother of two beautiful children, Jamir and Janai.

Made in the USA
Middletown, DE
10 September 2021